BLACK EMPLOYMENT

THE IMPACT OF RELIGION, ECONOMIC THEORY, POLITICS, AND LAW

D0998666

BLACK EMPLOYMENT
THE IMPACT OF RELIGION, ECONOMIC THEORY, POLITICS, AND LAW

IRVING KOVARSKY

CENTER FOR LABOR AND MANAGEMENT
COLLEGE OF BUSINESS ADMINISTRATION
THE UNIVERSITY OF IOWA

WILLIAM ALBRECHT

THE IOWA STATE UNIVERSITY PRESS ✾ AMES

CONTENTS ✂

FOREWORD

One of the major challenges of our times is to assist previously rejected men and women, the so-called "hard-core unemployed," toward productive employment. A substantial number of unemployed and underemployed Americans lack adequate education and job skills, particularly among Negroes, Mexican-Americans, Puerto Ricans, and Indians. This provocative and controversial monograph centers on one of the victimized groups, the plight of the black in the labor market.

Written from the standpoint of the black, this work by Professors Kovarsky and Albrecht interrelates history, constitutional issues, economic and social thought, religion, and legislative and judicial approaches to fair employment. The lucid style and interdisciplinary approach makes this monograph a significant contribution to the rapidly growing but still meager body of literature in this area.

On behalf of the College of Business Administration and its Center for Labor and Management, I express appreciation to those foundations and organizations whose interest and financial support have made this publication possible.

B. L. Barnes
Dean
College of Business Administration
The University of Iowa

PREFACE ❖

A review of the literature describing white racism and institutions all too often minimizes—a sign of impartiality if you will—the totality of the damage inflicted upon the black. A more realistic and honest approach would place greater emphasis upon white-inflicted injury to the black. Only in this fashion can more members of the white community begin to appreciate the radical black position today. Not until the damage and irrational hatred directed at the black is fully appreciated can meaningful communication between black and white take place. Gestures of good will are wasted unless the white community fully appreciates its responsibilities.

Sartre, describing the French attitude toward Algeria seeking its independence, establishes the tone for this manuscript:

> The "liberals" are stupified; they admit that we were not polite enough to the natives, that it would have been wiser and fairer to allow them certain rights in so far as this was possible; they ask nothing better than to admit them in batches and without sponsors to that very exclusive club, our species. . . . The Left at home (France) is embarrassed; they know the true situation of the natives, the merciless oppression they are submitted to; they do not condemn their revolt, knowing full well that we have done everything to provoke it. But, all the same, they think to themselves, there are limits. . . . Sometimes the Left scolds them. . . . "You're going too far; we won't support you any more." The natives don't give a damn about their support; for all the good it does them they might as well stuff it up their backsides. . . .[1]

Many blacks view the ghettos in the United States as colonies and hold in contempt both the conservative and liberal white viewpoints. This manuscript was prepared, hopefully, with some appreciation of the white damage inflicted upon the black.

William Albrecht
Irving Kovarsky
College of Business Administration
The University of Iowa

CHAPTER ONE ✂ AN OVERVIEW

Exploitation of the black in the United States has been the rule, not the exception. Social, legal, political, economic, and religious discrimination, in the deadening language of these callings, was the black heritage. Removed from Africa against his will, black adaptation to a foreign and hostile culture would have been difficult under the best of circumstances. Labeled inferior and religiously damned and shunted, the black after the Civil War was told privately and publicly to shift for himself in a society unwilling to accept or understand him. To have survived in this environment is tribute to the patience and stamina of the black.

The black in this country has been more cruelly exploited than elsewhere; at least the black in Colonial Africa was familiar with terrain, people, and customs. The black in the United States faced more hostility than the black in Brazil and Cuba where integration and acceptance, while imperfect, were commonplace. Hawaii, a "Johnny-come-lately" to statehood, holds a mix of native, Filipino, Chinese, and white, and integration is an accepted way of life.[2] The black in the United States has not "melted," prospered, or been accepted.

The formation of the United States as a nation rings with idealism and general high purpose, and our history books point to the colonial resentment of British rule. Colonial realists and utopian dreamers paved the way for a national philosophy which, on paper, worshipped equality and religious freedom. The prevailing spirit at the time of the Revolutionary War acknowledged the inalienable and natural rights of man, taking a cue from Greek philosophers and religion. While natural-right theory benefited handsomely most white citizens, particularly the Protestant, it did nothing for the black. Being part of an overwhelming majority, the white Protestant was in a position to assure respect for his rights. In fact, due to the common religious heritage of the white, denying the non-Protestant his just due was difficult. But, ah, the black man was another story.

Today, the white Protestant and others who have prospered are not convinced that the black has been denied opportunity for spurious reasons. In the rural North, the black is virtually unknown and the white community cannot appreciate the black push or attitude. Some of the white *avant-garde* groups dotting the college campus, a small band of disorganized lib-

1

erals, recognize the justice of the black position. But this recognition is seldom articulated in a manner acceptable to middle-class America—violence and other methods of demonstration are unacceptable to them. As a result, some white support has peeled away, unable to understand or accept black militancy.

To racists and the middle group, the disinterested and "neutral," the traumatic events of recent years—rioting, looting, struggle for political power, advocacy of a separate black community or nation—fortify preconceived notions that the black cannot be integrated into the white community. Even the liberal expresses doubt. Politicians, jurists, economists and educators refuse or are unable to understand the nature of the black revolt, a revolt that seeks far-reaching and immediate reform. Revolutionary rather than evolutionary changes must take place in white attitudes if future turmoil is to be minimized. The "fair-minded" white seeks evolutionary change while the black militant pushes for revolutionary change, both sides unable to avoid head-on clash. But far-reaching changes, these "giant" steps, will not take place unless pacesetters in our society—lawyers, politicians, religious leaders, economists, and others—recognize that concessions bordering on the trivia or geared to long-haul improvement are unacceptable and unfair to the young and militant black.

Institutional slavery ended with the Civil War, but the black has never shed his "badge of servitude." The adjective "slave" signifies more than the legal ownership of a human being; it also means hard and unpleasant work, total domination of a person, a drudge, etc., descriptions fitting the black today. Only one aspect of slavery—the legal ownership of the black—has ended. In all other respects, the black feels and resents the heavy hand of his white oppressor.

Full access to the job market has always been denied to the black. Economic prejudice was openly practiced in the South, while discrimination slightly more subtle closed doors to the Northern black with equal intensity. Most blacks lived in the rural South when the Civil War ended, where industry was virtually unknown and resented. Making the transition from slavery to freedom was bound to be difficult even if the path was strewn with roses—most blacks could not read or write, only a few were skilled craftsmen, families had been cruelly separated, and few friends could be turned to for meaningful help.

In addition to the critical period of adjustment that the freed black would encounter, the backbone of the southern economy, mainly cotton, was "shot" at the end of the Civil War. The black, even if educated and trained, could not find employment in the South in the absence of industry. Little imagination is needed to forecast the considerable economic difficulty the black would face. Freedom for the black was bound to be something different from freedom for the white—prejudice in the North and South and the absence of long-range planning spelled disaster for the black.

During World Wars I and II, the black left the rural South for urban centers in the North and South, searching for economic opportunity. Some employers actively recruited in the rural South during wartime, promising economic reward commensurate with ability and permanent opportunity. Employment opportunities were advertised by word of mouth through family and friend; in fact success stories of soul brothers in the big city reached the hinterland. The mention of indoor plumbing, running water, electricity, gas, and a refrigerator was enough to spur black migration to the city. Few blacks bothered to consider whether employment would be available on a nondiscriminatory basis—escape from the rural, poverty-stricken South was enough incentive.

What began as a rural and somewhat hidden shame—90 per cent of the black population lived in the rural South when the Civil War ended—turned gradually to an urban and visible concern in the North and South.[3] While living in isolated pockets in the South, black discontent was not patently visible. It is difficult to unite people into a significant power structure when families are widely scattered and without effective political leadership. In the urban center, black discontent and hostility surfaced after World War II. As of 1960, 20.5 million or 11 per cent of the total population in the United States was nonwhite.[4] Total population will expand by 41 per cent between 1960 and 1985, with the nonwhite segment increasing 68 per cent and the white segment increasing by 37 per cent.[5] During the same time span, nonwhite population in metropolitan areas will increase by 13.8 million or 104 per cent. In city centers, nonwhites will increase from 10.4 million in 1960 to 20.1 million by 1985.[6] By 1985, 75 per cent of all nonwhites will live in major cities while whites stream into the suburb. With the heavy concentration of black people in the city, disturbances are more visible and, evidently, far more effective than in the rural South. For this reason, the leadership of Martin Luther King, Jr. and Malcolm X was effective.

The promised Nirvana in the big city, typically north of the Mason-Dixon line, was a bubble that burst quickly. Some moving to the city improved their lot, finding the initial employment opportunity. Others moving to the city were less fortunate, experiencing difficulty finding jobs and housing. The black finding employment soon compared his bounty to white brethren —obviously, crumbs only, the less desirable jobs, were thrown his way. By word of mouth from long-term residents of the ghetto and observing differences between that available to him and whitey, black dissatisfaction mounted. The black in the urban North and West soon found no more, and sometimes less, respect in his new environment than in the

3

South. The impersonality, pace, and lack of communication between city people further alienated the newcomer. Disenchantment was complete when on the job he could not aspire to promotion and was the first to be laid off. Opportunity and self-respect were denied the black male who was expected to provide for his family.

In turn, the white community could not fathom the dissatisfaction and way of life of the black. White citizens, some less prejudiced than others, ignored the obvious—that the black yardstick of well-being was now based on city standards rather than those generally prevailing in the rural South. Blacks came out of an environment calling for black docility to maximize success, and whites in the large city could not understand the lack of black aggressiveness in industry. Where aggressiveness was exhibited, this was soon squelched by the white competitor.

The meaning of equality and justice is pertinent at this point. That all men are created equal and function in a society dedicated to equality is unadulterated hogwash, a fact of life better understood in the ghetto than in the middle- and upper-class neighborhoods. Rather than mouthing, like a broken record, meaningless, shopworn, and empty promises that can never be fulfilled, society, to assure the greatest range of opportunity, must establish a framework in which social, economic, and political barriers that hinge on background and race are removed. All men, not even large segments of our society, cannot be precisely equal, but it is desirable, and perhaps possible, to function in a manner which dignifies those seeking opportunity.

The public is aware that the black has been shamefully treated; whether the white is ready to make amends is another question. If amends are in order, the spark will come from urban and northern centers of population, spurred by black and white alike. Where the black resides in large numbers, his political power together with the interests of city-oriented whites make possible a coalition. The rural North and white South do not feel responsible or have no need to promote the well-being of the black; the rural North seldom sees the black while southern attitudes are more complex, unchanged since the Civil War. The northern and urban white abhors black tactics promoting change and feels that more cannot be accomplished in the short run to help the black without injury to the white. Confrontation between black and white is inevitable in the big city; thus, the strong push to resolve differences based on white fear and black need will have to come from that quarter. Where aid is extended because of centuries of black need and white fear, resolution comes with great difficulty. If the moral commitment on the part of the white community were greater, solution would be less difficult.

If representation in Congress and state assemblies was more evenly distributed on the basis of population, which means loss of power for the rural resident and more voice for the suburb and city, city problems would receive greater priority.[7] The Supreme Court has told the state legislatures that representation must follow population—that the rural areas are disproportionately represented—but progress toward equal representation has been slow. Today, cities are more equally represented because of the white migration to the suburb. This means that the political power of the city black has increased, while the suburb is underrepresented and the rural community overrepresented. While the middle-class and influential white has fled to the suburb, he supports extending a helping hand to the city because the destinies of these contiguous areas are interwoven.

A good look at black leadership today is essential to develop programs necessary to give the black his just due. The black of the past, inwardly seething but outwardly calm, should be toasted by the white. To have been patient this long is proof of self-control and some faith in white institutions. The white view of the black as a jovial, shuffling, and irresponsible child, looking for a good time on Saturday and repenting on Sunday, has to be laid to rest. The metropolitan white making casual contact with the black knows that his patience (and fear) have ended—a walk through any ghetto should convince the skeptic of black hatred for the white. For this reason and others, the metropolitan white needs little convincing that the city must be helped. It may be wise to assume that the black community, even its conservative leaders, is committed to or accepts violence or disruption as necessary to assure change. While the conservative black does not endorse violence openly—he could lose his source of power by tipping his hand—he supports force more than is conceded. To the young and militant black, white support is not a critical factor: as stated by Sartre, "(F)or all the good it does them (blacks) they (whites) might as well stuff it up their backsides."

Black organization and leadership continue to improve, and the vocal and militant leader has been replacing the older and more conservative black leader. The more conservative leader operates at a disadvantage since the changes taking place cannot be attributed to his tactics—he could be forced to exhibit militancy to maintain his leadership role. If "signs" are read correctly, the black community will be less constrained in the future. Many black leaders already believe that time has run out and that the black and white must live apart as equals. But it still comes as a surprise—and here is where hope lies—that large numbers of blacks reject the philosophy of a Garvey, the Black Muslims, or the Black Panthers.

More than a few blacks are convinced that time is not on their side—and history supports this position—and that the white devil can be taken off the black back only by guerrilla warfare. It is unfortunate that white political, economic, social, and legal leaders fail to sense fully the black mood. The academician and jurist, content to wait and trained to respond slowly, too often ignore change taking place under their noses. If necessary, the black community can be controlled by military tactics, a fact accepted by black militant leaders. Nevertheless, white military supremacy is poor justification to prevent the black from living in dignity. If friction is to be reduced, the black must be permitted to call part of the tune while the white bows gracefully to his new social partner. Instead, the white community treats violence as a black characteristic and ignores any responsibility for it. The white community abhors violence (except when practiced by it) but overlooks what might be lumped together as continued white-collar crime against the black community.

However inconsequential in terms of need, changes are taking place in our political, economic, religious, and judicial philosophies. Help to the black is being extended slowly and reluctantly, help unfortunately denied after the Civil War ended. Should educators, ministers, legislators, and jurists swing the big hammer at discrimination rather than aim the powder-puff blow, more wrongs could be righted. But these centers of power and the public are not convinced that a big stick must be wielded to atone for past and present injustice. If the public backs more meaningful programming, the next step is to convince the black community of white sincerity. Stop-gap and halfway measures are not meaningful—partial measures only fan black ambition, whose leaders are aware that small chinks have already been made in the all-white armor. Halfway measures only point to the insincerity of the white community. It is entirely possible that emotional fervor and dedication are more essential than the approach of the cool "intellect."

This manuscript has been prepared for the purpose of interrelating black history, constitutional issues, economic and social thought, religion, and the legislative and judicial approaches to fair employment. Hopefully, the interdisciplinary approach will more forcefully demonstrate past injury to the black and the need to adopt policies calculated to induce meaningful change.

CHAPTER TWO ❧ A SHORT HISTORY
OF THE BLACK

Dr. Louis Leakey in 1959 discovered in East Africa the fossil of a tool-maker, who lived about 1.5 million years ago. Africa may have been the birthplace of man since the prior earliest known fossil, the Peking man, dates much later. Toolmaking, which is basic to the evolution of man, might have originated on the black continent. There is substantial evidence pointing to the rich culture of the black in Africa. The popular misconception of black heritage is due to prejudice, ignorance of history, and misunderstanding of the term "primitive." A primitive society is often equated with a backward society rather than, as the term denotes, a static and isolated society as opposed to a dynamic and expansive culture.

Specialization was common in Africa as skilled craftsmen produced fine examples of iron working, weaving, wood carving, pottery, bronze casting, etc.[8] In fact, the ancient black was skilled in the arts known today (there is no record of painting since it was practiced on sand, leaving no permanent record); some African craftsmanship, sculpting, gold, glass, clay, silver, pottery, etc., was outstanding.[9] The earliest known pottery was made in Africa during the Paleolithic Age. And contrary to the heathenistic label stamped upon blacks in Colonial America and subsequently, much of the primitive art, like the face mask and sculpture, shows considerable concern with religion and ancestor worship.

The primitive artist was obsessed with geometric expression and abstraction, art forms which were not brought into the white world until the twentieth century.[10] The Cubist movement, led by Picasso and Braque during the early Twentieth Century, was influenced by African art. The black influence can be seen in Picasso's famous painting "The Ladies of Avignon," in which cubic blocks and hollowed-out shapes are prominent.[11] Van Gogh and Gauguin were also influenced by primitive art.

Although few African tribes reduced spoken language to writing before the Civil War—to some an indication of an inferior human order—speech patterns often indicated a rich heritage. Mario Pei points to the Swahili language as evidence of a rich culture.[12]

Family life in black Africa was stable; although polygamy was practiced, the family formed a strong unit in tribal life. Blacks in Africa were among the first to engage in farming.

7

In the third millenium before Christ, Ra Nahesi, a black, occupied the Egyptian throne. Nefertiti, the wife of Ahmose I, was a black of considerable beauty and talent. Through her, the Egyptian aristocracy was infused with Negro blood. After the Ethiopian Pharaohs conquered Egypt, intermarriage between citizens of these nations was common, leading to a fusion of race and culture.[13]

Following the practice of the day, Egyptians held slaves—Semites, Mediterraneans, and blacks from Ethiopia.[14] The Hebrews held slaves. After the Mohammedan invasion of Africa, the black woman was locked in the harem, undertaking the role of an attendant or wife, while the black male was pressed into the military or used as a household servant. During this period of Semitic importance, the slave was not used to produce wealth, representing instead social status.

White and black slaves were common in ancient Greece. In some of the city-states, half of the population were slaves, kidnaped from the East and North or captured in war.[15] Plato suggests that slavery is the common denominator for all mankind since every family could point to an ancestor in bondage.[16] Greeks rationalized the enslavement of intellectual inferiors to relieve the thinking man, naturally a Greek, from necessary drudgery which did not require intelligence. Plato, in the *Republic*, accepts slavery as a way of life. In the *Laws*, Plato spells out the treatment that the slave is entitled to. Manumission was common, whether black or white, and the freed person became an integral part of society.

Romans rationalized slavery as an implied agreement resulting from war wherein the military victor was entitled to the services of the vanquished. The success of the Roman military led to the return of the high-placed soldier with sizable fortune who bought up small farms, consolidating them into a large agricultural unit. The slave, while unprofitable on the small farm, could be used profitably the year around on the large farm.[17] As a result, slaves labored in significant number on the large Roman farm.

To set the record straight, prejudice was common in the Greek city-state and in the Roman Empire. For example, Jews and Greeks disliked each other. While admiring the toughness of the barbaric German, Caesar fanned hatred against them.[18] Yet prejudice against the barbarian could be softened because the Roman and German did not separate—an exclusive white club was not established. Since the German emulated the Roman, racial prejudice was waylaid, permitting token acceptance by the dominant society. Hatred against the Jew, on the other hand, was always extensive since he wished to maintain a separate identity rather than accept the way of life of his oppressor.

Compare the Greek and Roman attitude toward slavery with that in the United States. While profit was small and many slaves white, Greek and

Roman citizens never held the slave in as low esteem as did our citizens. The black slave in the United States was always viewed as a member of an inferior order. As observed by de Tocqueville:

> The ancients kept the bodies of their slaves in bondage, but placed no restraints upon the mind and no check upon education; and they acted consistently with their established principle, since a natural termination of slavery then existed, and one day or other the slave might be set free and become the equal of his masters. But . . . the South . . . (which) did not admit that the Negroes can ever be commingled with themselves, have forbidden them, under severe penalties, to be taught to read or write. . . .[19]

Under Greek and Roman law, a family could adopt a slave, entitling him to citizenship. The slave protected by Roman law, a noncitizen, was less likely to be treated as an article of property than under Greek law because of the incorporation of the concepts of Natural Law into the Roman Law.[20] The Roman Natural Law eulogized the dignity of man, turning to philosophy or religion as justification, an approach which contradicts slavery. The law followed in Colonial America was inherited from England, which did not provide for the protection of the slave. Sir Henry Maine speculates that:

> (t)here is a great deal of evidence that in those American States which have taken the highly Romanised code of Louisiana as the basis of their jurisprudence, the lot and prospects of the Negro population were better in many material respects, until the letter of the fundamental law was overlaid by recent statutory enactments . . . than under institutions founded on the English Common Law, which . . . has no true place for the Slave, and can only regard him as a chattel.[21]

After the Norman conquest of England, slavery increased, but the sale of slaves to other countries was forbidden by statute due to the influence of the Christian Church.[22]

Few black slaves could be found in Western Europe until the end of the fourteenth century. By 1460, 700 to 800 black slaves were brought to Portugal each year. The Portuguese rulers of this era viewed slavery as the fulfillment of a holy cause—the black was a heathen—a view pushed by the *religioso*. Because of the tight rein of the monarchs and the considerable influence of church leaders, black slavery was introduced into European life. The fact that Black Africa was preoccupied with religion and mysticism was of no consequence to Christian Europe.

The need for the slave in Europe was insignificant when measured by his use on the southern plantation in the United States. Furthermore, profits from working slaves in the United States were huge, while economic gain in Europe was limited, except for a slave trader. In the New World, the supply of labor was limited while labor was plentiful in England after the land enclosures.[23] Under the English system of villeinage, white people born into

9

poverty who would not improve their economic lot, and indentured servants assured a sufficient and cheap supply of labor.[24]

Although blacks did not accompany the English into the New World, they did carry the banners of Spain and Portugal across the sea; these blacks came to Spain and Portugal with the Islamic invasion. While the Spanish black was initially forbidden entry into the New World, the ban was lifted in 1501. Blacks followed Balboa, Cortez, Pizarro, De Soto, and others into America. Blacks helped to conquer and settle Peru; a Spanish black, Estevanico, helped to settle New Mexico and Arizona. The first settler in the Chicago area was probably black. On the Nina, the flagship sailed by Columbus, a black served as pilot.[25] Blacks accompanied Jesuit missionaries into Canada.

While Portugal was the first nation to exploit the slave trade in America, the large traders during the seventeenth and eighteenth centuries were Dutch, French, and English. After Spain and England signed the Treaty of Utrecht in 1713, the notorious Royal African Company of England monopolized the slave trade in the colonies.[26] In a ten-year span, from 1783 to 1793, traders from Liverpool imported 303,737 slaves into the colonies.[27]

Portugal shipped slaves to Brazil.[28] In fact, between five and eighteen million blacks were brought to Brazil between 1528 and 1828.[29] Influenced by Roman law and Catholicism, manumission and the education of the black was encouraged rather than forbidden. Black women giving birth to ten children were freed in Brazil. Other reasons advanced for differences in attitude between the Brazilian and colonist were that the black brought to Brazil was culturally superior to the white and Indian inhabitant[30] and that the Portuguese settler was less prejudiced.[31] In any event, what is abhorred as the mongrelization of races in the United States was accepted in Brazil; intermarriage between white and black, often due to a shortage of women, was commonplace.[32]

A claim is made that there are two distinct patterns of racial prejudice. An alien culture faces prejudice because its customs are different and attempts are made at isolation.[33] Discrimination against the Jew is an example of this type of prejudice.[34] A second pattern of discrimination is based on the political and economic competition that the "foreigner" brings.[35] In the city-state and Rome, apparently the dominant reason for the prejudice directed against the Jew was his aloofness. But this wall also spared the Jew from some prejudice since he was not a political (and economic) threat to the Greek and Roman majority. Later, because of religious differences, prejudice directed against the Jew increased; it is religion and economic gain that fan hatred. But the black did not seek separation—he was isolated by a white society—and he was not an economic or political

10

threat. Because of color and different customs, the white feared and hated the black.

The first blacks brought to the English colonies were captured by a Dutch ship, an act of piracy, en route to white owners and mistakenly taken to Jamestown, Virginia, instead of the West Indies. The blacks in the colonies were treated as freemen, and Johnson, one of the blacks, later became a slaveholder.[36] In fact, blacks, for the initial forty to one hundred years, were freemen.[37]

Colonists imported indentured servants and convicts from England during the seventeenth and eighteenth centuries to bolster the meager supply of labor. It is estimated that one-half of the colonists were convicts or indentured servants.[38] Unfortunately for the black, the convict and indentured servant proved unsatisfactory to the employer. Many convicts and indentured workers were untrustworthy, and settlers feared the convict. The contract of indenture, usually for a seven-year period, was often uneconomic. Transporting laborers and their families from England was costly, since only the head of the family contracted to work. Working time was lost while the new arrival and his family adjusted to the Southern climate. With labor in short supply, wages in the colonies moved upward. With falling agricultural prices and tax increases, the employer, unable to substitute technology for manpower, turned to the reduction of labor costs.[39] But the political, legal, and social climate in the colonies prevented squeezing the white worker too ruthlessly.

The South was ill-suited to small-scale farming, and the large farm required a large supply of unskilled labor. The large planters ultimately agreed that the English system of labor was not profitable in the colonies. The black slave, without economic and political influence and unable to turn to a religious organization for protection, was a logical scapegoat— slave labor was being used successfully in South America; tribal leaders in Africa were willing to sell blacks accustomed to heat and working in fields; and the English legal structure adopted in the South neither prohibited slavery nor protected slaves.[40] Slaves were profitably utilized, from about 1690, to cultivate rice, cotton, and indigo in South America.[41] Tobacco growers in the colonies gambled, importing the black, and his status shifted slowly from freeman to slave.[42] The experiment was a gamble because slavery was unsuccessful in the colonies before planters turned to the black; the earliest record of slavery is 1637 when Indians captured in New England were forced to work by their captors.[43] The Indian slave was unable to adapt to farm routine and, in addition, proved susceptible to disease while in captivity. Furthermore, planters in Virginia tried the Indian as an indentured servant without success.[44]

11

Black slaves could be found in the South during the seventeenth century, but not until the end of the eighteenth century did slavery become an important economic, political, and social institution.[45] Planters in Virginia and Maryland did not seek slave labor during the seventeenth century, attributable, at least partially, to a familiarity with the English system of villeinage. In fact, for some time after the Revolutionary War, slave labor proved uneconomic in the South; but the black was not freed because the colonist feared him. From 1840, the number of slaves in the South increased geometrically.[46]

Slavery in the North expired noiselessly. In Pennsylvania, the slave was educated and given freedom of locomotion, an advantage seldom bestowed in the southern state.[47] Furthermore, marriage and the black family were respected by the northern slaveholder. The influence of a religious institution and a simple economic fact of life ended slavery in Pennsylvania; the Quaker was dead set against slavery, and the small businessman and farmer could not use the slave to economic advantage.

Benjamin Franklin's scale of preferences placed the farmer above the small businessman. Franklin argued that the farmer produces new wealth whereas the industrialist only changes the form of goods, adding to and taking away from its original value.[48] For this reason, the farmer was a more valuable citizen. Since farms and industry were small in Pennsylvania, Franklin also reasoned that slave labor was more expensive than free labor. According to Franklin, slavery was favored by those wanting to stop labor turnover, thereby avoiding competition from a former employee.[49]

Slavery was doomed in the northern colonies when the Revolutionary War began. The number of slaves in New England dropped from 13,000 to 3,700 by 1790.[50] In 1800, 36,505 slaves were located in the North, mainly in New York and New Jersey.[51] Slavery ended by constitutional fiat in Vermont (1777), Ohio (1802), Illinois (1818), and Indiana (1816); by judicial decision in Massachusetts (1783) and New Hampshire (1783); and by legislation in Pennsylvania (1780), Rhode Island (1784), Connecticut (1784, 1797), New York (1799, 1817), and New Jersey (1804).

While slavery was inhuman, profit and the potential political and economic threat to the white prevented its demise in the South. Without profit, slavery ended in the North without struggle. Furthermore, few slaves were in the North when compared to the South. Other reasons assigned for the painless end of slavery in the North are:

1. The slave could not adapt to the cold.
2. The black, intellectually backward, could not learn more than tending to one crop.
3. The colonist in the Revolutionary War fought to end oppressive taxation and lack of representation in the English Parliament. This spirit of equality

and fairness was linked to the Roman concept of Natural Law, calling for justice for all men. Thus, the prevailing ideology called for the termination of slavery. Although the same revolutionary spirit prevailed North and South, the large profit reaped from cotton after the invention of the cotton gin and the fear of the slaves in the South prevented a peaceful solution.[52]

While rice, tobacco, and indigo constituted the dominant crops, slave-holding increased slowly. Clothing made of cotton was a sign of poverty in England, and its use, consequently, was restricted. Cotton became fashionable as apparel after the Industrial Revolution in England. Textile manufacturers in England seized the opportunity to reap fortunes and profits were unusually large when the demand for cotton clothing continued to mount. When the cotton gin was invented in 1794 to remove seed from the short fiber, the profit potential for the grower improved. Four years after the gin was introduced, cotton production in the United States doubled.[53] As cotton productivity increased, so did the number of slaves. By 1850, approximately 60 per cent of all slaves worked on cotton plantations.

After the Industrial Revolution began in England, Parliament passed a law abolishing slavery in all affiliated territories[54] with owners to be compensated by the Crown, a procedure recommended by President Lincoln before the Civil War. The Acts of 1807 and 1811 in England prohibited slave trading.[55]

Anticipated profit from cotton led to further exploitation of the Indian. After General Andrew Jackson and his army defeated the Creeks, the Indians were moved because the land was suitable to grow cotton.

Cotton consumption in the United States was large by 1840. In addition, the South supplied Great Britain with 82 per cent of its cotton and Europe with three-fourths of its supply. These economic facts point to differences between northern and southern businessmen. New England, interested in protecting a young and inefficient manufacturing industry, favored tariffs, while the South, in deference to shipping interests in Charleston and cotton growers, advocated free trade.[56]

Some labor economists and historians maintain that a coalition between black freemen and poor whites was a natural solution to problems faced by both. It is unlikely that black freemen and white serfs could develop economic comradery in a short time. The black and white sprang from cultures having little in common; dress, customs, goals, and religious heritage were entirely different. White settlers came to the colonies as a family unit or quickly formed one, while the black was kidnaped, destroying his family structure in the process. The European in the New World was exclusively motivated by financial gain while the black came from a society where communal rather than individual ownership was practiced, leading to different economic values. Consequently, black and white alike would need time to bridge the economic and social gulf. The profit to be squeezed from cotton signaled an end to the slim possibility of an amalgamation of black and white interests. Furthermore, by 1790, four years before Eli Whitney perfected the cotton gin, 19 per cent of the population was black, a political threat to the white.[57] Southern politicians endorsed the constitutional prohibition against slave importation from Africa, fearing the black mass.[58]

de Tocqueville accurately forecast that:

> The Indians will perish in the same isolated conditions in which they have lived, but the destiny of the Negro is in some measure interwoven with that of the Europeans. These two races are fastened to each other without intermingling; and they are alike unable to separate entirely or to combine.[59]

The Indian "problem" was resolved easily; unable to acclimate to white ways and labor, the white community stripped him of land and pushed him aside. For a long time, official policy in the United States was aimed at containing the Indian on a squalid reservation. But the southern planter needed the black, preventing total separation between black and white. Because "the destiny of the Negro" was "in some measure interwoven with that of the Europeans," white antagonism against the black became more pronounced than against the Indian.

de Tocqueville also observed:

> Whoever has inhabited the United States must have perceived that in those parts of the Union in which the Negroes are no longer slaves they have in no wise drawn nearer to the whites. On the contrary, the prejudice of race appears to be stronger in the states that have abolished slavery than in those where it still exists; and nowhere is it so intolerant as in those states where servitude has never been known.[60]

> If I were called upon to predict the future, I should say that the abolition of slavery in the South will . . . increase the repugnance of the white population for the blacks. . . .[61]

CHAPTER THREE ⅔ THE CLOSING IN

Residents of the New World, while showing signs of being uncomfortable, rationalized slavery in many ways. That slavery continued in the South after petering out in the North requires more explanation than a fear of freeing the black and the huge profit of the planter. Citizens certain of the righteous path and what is best for society share responsibility with the slaveowner for the perpetuation of an evil system. Religious leaders, economists, politicians, and jurists, all following a common goal, are four callings that contributed substantially to the black downfall. These four groups, the educated elite and leaders of the day, with few exceptions justified or ignored slavery. Although fear and profit were the springboard, the slaveholder needed the *religioso*, economist, politician, and jurist to continue the barbarous system.

The purpose of this section is to explain and spotlight the inhumanity that was exhibited and point to the professional explanations resorted to by men of the cloth, economists, politicians, and jurists. No attempt is made here to justify the views of these professions; the literature is full of explanations. Attitudes being what they were (and are), prejudice takes hold and learned justifications are often resorted to as a cover for an unwillingness to "rock the boat."

Religion

Slavery in the United States initially was condoned for religious reasons, that the black was a heathen, not one of God's children, or he had to be shown the "righteous path." Many colonists were Protestant dissenters from England; having known intolerance in England, popular myth circulates that religious tolerance was common among the colonial settlers. Although some tolerance was practiced, it must be viewed from the perspective of a predominantly Protestant population. Only 3,000 Jews and 300,000 Catholics, out of a total population of 3,000,000, lived in the colonies at the outbreak of the Revolutionary War.[62] Minorities always experience degrees of social, political, and economic difficulty in a pecking order favoring the dominant religion, in this case Protestantism. But the tendency to discriminate against white minorities is partially and at least temporarily checked by the sharing of a common religious heritage and experience.

15

The black was forcibly, illegally, brought to the colonies, and his look and way of life were enough to lead settlers to conclude that the black was cut from a different mold. Under such circumstances, it was "logical" to treat the black as a heathen. More accurately, a religious flock more easily accepts the external trappings of a "foreign" religion that they are familiar with. The black brought to the colonies had been exposed to religion, but it was religion that the whites could not tolerate or understand; at best it was viewed as black magic. Certainly the black was concerned with mysticism, gods, evil spirits, etc.[63] In fact, the more primitive the community, the greater its concern with religion.

The great religious literature known to the white world seldom mentions race; rather, there are references to nations, tribes, and tongues, indicative of an awareness of differences between groups.[64] In fact, well-defined concepts of racial superiority were absent until developed by the French diplomat, Comte Arthur de Gobineau; his racial theory was based to a large degree on differences between the aristocrat and commoner in Europe.[65]

Being black and unaccepting of or unexposed to white values explain the heathen label and the consequential stamp of inferiority. Intolerance may be more natural than acceptance, and differences in religion too often fan prejudice. Religion had been used to justify white inhumanity to white, and the black was a natural "pigeon" for this brand of intolerance; in fact, swinging a religious club against the black was easier than against the white "heretic." Although treated in New England as a freeman, the absence of religion in the black justified the label of inferiority and, later, slavery. Had the black arrived in the New World as a Catholic, Jew, or Protestant, other reasons to justify prejudice would have been advanced. In fact, some slaves were Moslems, a respected and "acceptable" religion; their lot was no different from the black heathen's.

While the black was a slave, racial theories were unnecessary to explain the inferiority of the black. The fact that explanations were resorted to is indicative of the ambivalent feeling in the white community toward slavery.

A few religious leaders, notably northern Quakers and southern Catholics, weakly condemned slavery or the treatment accorded the slave. The Quaker antipathy toward slavery was based on the notion that God resides in all men, and no one should live luxuriously because another is denied his freedom. The Catholic religion, latching onto Roman law and ways, found unfair the status accorded the black. Impotent in the South before the Civil War, Catholic clergymen at least insisted upon baptism and religious instruction for the black to help ease the pain. But most religious leaders in the North and South accepted or refused to condemn slavery. This lack of appreciation for different religions sometimes manifests itself today. For example, not one leader from another denomination stepped forward to support the Jehovah's Witnesses and Unitarian Church when they were denied tax exemption several years ago in Los Angeles.[66]

William Penn was more generous than other religious leaders, believing that the slave was entitled to freedom after fourteen years. On the other hand, Cotton Mather felt that God blessed his family when given a slave.[67] Oliver Cromwell, the Puritan leader in England, sold into slavery in Barbados all of the Irish that were not killed in the Drogheda massacre.[68]

Gradually, Protestant sects in the South, particularly Baptists and Methodists, turned their attention to saving the black soul. A strange theology indeed was practiced when religious leaders condoning slavery sought salvation for the black. The black entered the Baptist and Methodist fold at the end of the seventeenth century, religions then appealing to the poor black and white. When conversion to Christianity began, baptism of the black was legal ground for freedom.[69] Consequently, state laws were changed; for example, Virginia in 1667 enacted a law declaring that baptism would not bring freedom to the black. Not until 1790, or thereabouts, did discrimination become overt and doctrinaire in the churches.[70] Prominent ministers in the South, with scarcely a contrary ripple, vocally supported slavery.[71]

Some southern clergymen solicited black membership to assure better treatment that a Christian would be entitled to. Not only was religion a spiritual comfort, but the master would be morally obligated to treat the slave with care and civility. Many ministers were consumed by an occupational hazard—the call of the cloth—to "enlighten" the black. Nevertheless, planters feared religious instruction for the black because the relationship between master and slave would change; biblical lore, particularly the story of Moses and the Jews escaping from slavery in Egypt,[72] would whet the imagination of the black; permitting the black to assemble was dangerous to the white; and a little education for the black endangered the southern way of life.[73]

The church rationale advanced to support slavery is interesting. Through selective misuse, the Bible can be quoted to support segregation and integration. There is a great deal of similarity between legal and religious analysis—any position can be supported by turning to the "good book." Segregationists referred to Genesis 9:25, the curse placed by Noah on the Canaanites destined for slavery. Puritans in New England supported slavery because blacks had been cursed and now they could be led to God.[74] Pointing to the Mosaic Code, which mentions slavery, church leaders claimed endorsement from Above. Others claimed that slavery was a political rather than a religious issue, excusing involvement from religious quarters.[75] To divide spheres of authority between politics and religion where the slave was concerned must have led to a few sleepless nights for the more sensitive representatives of the cloth.

Recalling agonizing experiences in Europe, political and religious separation, the Jeffersonian "wall," seemed desirable to the colonial; furthermore, pushing for religious equality can be easier when political and religious leadership are separated. The religious leader who fears political interference is a realist; to support a "hands-off" policy from the political is desirable. The defect in this stand is that the religion which keeps out of the political mainstream loses influence and followers (we recognize that followers are sometime gained). Actually, religious leaders have been accustomed to "throwing their weight" about to solve important issues. To stop political involvement in behalf of the black was either a sign of indifference or fear that the church could not handle white hostility.

Can religion and politics be separated? Difficult decisions of trying to separate church and state can be pointed to, and, unquestionably, more constitutional agonizing is in the offing.[76] It appears easier for the state to stay out of church affairs than for the church to refrain from involvement in political issues even where separable. Religious leaders today often express the need for involvement in current affairs if church influence is to be kept alive. Church survival, if for no other reason, pushes its leaders into taking sides on important issues, even those that can be labeled political problems.

To this point, church and political affairs were treated as separable. There is much to be said for the position that the "wall" called for by Jefferson should be followed by the state, but it is difficult for the religious leader in good conscience to respect this barrier. How can there be separation from worldly and temporal matters unless, like the hippie, an attempt is made to withdraw from the mainstream?

Religion can never be completely divorced from the political; this is the most plausible position if religion is to be meaningful. Furthermore, the First Amendment protects the religious leader politically involved (but not within his church). The First Amendment fixing a "wall" between state and religion should have assuaged the fears of church officials and encouraged effort in behalf of the black. We can only conclude that member resentment was the chief concern of the minister rather than fear of the state or there was *religioso* approval of slavery.

Some church leaders opposed slavery without openly taking a stand. The Church Anti-Slavery League was established in the North in 1859, enlisting the support of Protestant clergymen believing that slavery must be abolished. However, the so-called radicalism of the organization and its position that slaveholding was sinful alienated most of the Northern clergy.[77] Even today ministers comment cautiously, if at all, on racial issues, fearing the middle-class syndrome. In fact, it is claimed that Sunday morning is the most segregated time of the week. As in every walk of life, success within the church—the size of the flock and assets—is measured. The minister serving a flock approving of slavery will antagonize parishioners by pointing to their immorality.[78] One church newspaper favored suppressing the abolitionist viewpoint, reasoning that "(n)o man has a moral right to use the power of speech in defiance of reason and revelation."[79]

Religion, or a lack thereof, is used to excuse inhumanity. Church doctrine throws some light on the callous attitude developed toward slavery. Luther carried many of the qualities of the peasant, finding virtue in people earning a living by physical labor, castigating the idle.[80] Luther did not favor economic equality since the spiritual kingdom would be exchanged for an earthly one. While the voracious economic appetite was not eulogized, Luther did not feel that religion should involve itself in the depths of the business world (Catholicism and Judaism in contrast favored church intervention in business to assure fair dealing). Luther's stand, unfortunately, allows the individual to regulate his business conduct without church condemnation. As stated by Tawney:

> It (the church) had insisted that all men were brethren. But it did not occur to it to point out that, as a result of the new economic imperialism which was beginning to develop in the seventeenth century, the brethren of the English merchant were the Africans whom he kidnapped for slavery in America, or the American Indians whom he stripped of their lands, or the Indian craftsmen from whom he bought muslin and silks at starvation prices. . . .[81]

Luther's philosophy did nothing to quell the appetite for material progress, and moral guidance was unavailable to the business world. Luther's approach was damaging to society because legal and political leaders of the day could not or would not provide moral leadership to protect the less fortunate in a changing society. Luther also believed that man's station in life was preordained and the individual must accept the cards dealt him.[82] Luther did not approve or disapprove of slavery in the name of God, but encouraging people to accept their destiny leads to an inference that slavery is preordained. Furthermore, Luther was strongly prejudiced against the Jew, and it is likely that he was similarly disposed toward the black.

Lutheranism followed the spirit of Malthus (and Ricardo to a lesser extent), an economic theorist who reasoned that in the long run most people can only expect to earn enough to survive. The black slave was cared for—after all, he represented an investment—and his survival was assured in a fashion similar to the poor white. Authorities in England often felt that the poor must remain poor or all industrial incentive would disappear. In fact, some felt that slavery was necessary to prevent idleness.[83]

Calvinist doctrine led to political struggle in England, France, and the Netherlands during the sixteenth and seventeenth centuries; followers of

19

Calvin came to the colonies from England, France, and the Netherlands. Calvin declared that the few chosen for external grace cannot be restricted by others. Thus, those not favored (like the black?) must accept their fate.[84] This was a harsh doctrine and a striking departure from Catholicism, despite the fact that Calvin was interested in saving man's soul and not in the promotion of business.

Weber contends that the spirit of capitalism

> was present before the capitalistic order. There were complaints of a peculiarly calculating sort of profit-seeking in New England . . . as early as 1632. It is further undoubted that capitalism remained far less developed in some of the neighbouring colonies, the later Southern States . . . in spite of the fact that these latter were founded by large capitalists for business motives, while the New England colonies were founded by preachers . . . with the help of small bourgeois, craftsmen, and yeomen, for religious reasons. . . .[85]

The Protestantism that developed in Europe conditioned spiritual leaders in the New World to let businessmen function without criticism, even though the black was bodily and spiritually restricted. Upon close examination, this Protestant ethic is curious indeed; that poverty should be accepted as the preordained way of life is really "interference," albeit acceptable interference, in the industrial sphere; but the imposition of ethical standards upon the employer was not for the clergy. The concept of "neutrality" is indeed shallow, a "neutrality" equaled by economists, politicians, and jurists.

Ministers following a policy of neutrality toed a dangerous line. Because the black was legally inferior—in fact, he did not have any rights under English and American law—neither a common law nor religiously sanctioned marriage could be contracted by the black. Based on Matthew, Chapter 19, Verse 6, "What God hath therefore joined together let no man put asunder," marriage was treated as indissoluble (annulment was permitted) and divorce intolerable. Prior to and after the Civil War, the common law marriage was accepted legally, marriages indissoluble to preserve the family unit. Except for the quirk in the law that they did not have any legally recognized rights (the position taken by the Supreme Court in the *Dred Scott* case, later reviewed), blacks lived together as husband and wife. Clergymen in the South raised little fuss when black families were separated by their white owners. When church doctrine promotes and protects marriage, the clergy should have protested the separation of the family. The clergy also knew that owners encouraged the mating of slaves to breed a new "crop."[86]

Failing to urge the keeping of the black family intact places responsibility on the Church not only for its support of slavery but for ignoring

20

church doctrine when expedient. Churchmen, relying on doctrine, should have stepped in to protect the black family in slavery. Churchmen took steps to prevent the passage of laws permitting divorce because of the holy sanctity of the marital contract. Whether a common law marriage is contracted is a question of fact; a common law marriage is defined as "one . . . created by an agreement to marry, followed by cohabitation. . . ."[87] It would seem that many blacks contracted common law marriages. Yet the southern clergy seldom spoke out against the sale of slaves, separating husband, wife, and children, destroying the family and encouraging promiscuity. But they waded into the battle to prevent the passage of laws permitting divorce. Furthermore, the southern clergy knew that slave owners in the North respected the family unit.[88] What "God hath put together" was indeed being pulled "asunder" by the master, and southern clergy batted nary an eye.[89]

In summation, slavery was accepted in the colonies because the black was a heathen. But such a deficiency is corrected after black initiation into Christianity. After black baptism, theologians resorted to history or theological doctrine to condone slavery. While more clergymen in the South were against slavery than the few condemning it, a predominant majority supported it. Today it is claimed that the South is the most basically Christian area in the United States.[90] Yet southern churches only reluctantly condemn discrimination against the black and remain the most segregated and inflexible. While said to be inseparable, morality and religion often are separable. A few years back, Martin Luther King, Jr. claimed that if southern church leaders took a stand, the killing of blacks and other brutality would quickly end. Dr. King claimed that business leaders in the South respond "much more quickly from economic considerations than do churchmen from moral considerations."[91]

Classical Economic Theory

The number of slaves in the United States grew from less than 300,000 in 1776 to 4,000,000 in 1860.[92] It was during this period that the Industrial Revolution started in England and in parts of the United States. It was during this period that "classical economics" became the dominant economic philosophy in the two countries. Both of these developments significantly affected the status of the black American.

Up to the latter part of the eighteenth century, the eve of the American Revolution and Industrial Revolution in England, the vast majority of the world's population was poor. Most people lived in what, by any reasonable definition, would be classified as poverty. Even as late as the medieval period, 99 per cent of the population was poor.[93] Only in the past several hundred years, which constitute a small portion of man's history, have

21

nations housed a significant percentage of people escaping a life of poverty. By the nineteenth century, the incomes of 25 to 35 per cent of the English and American people had risen above the poverty level.[94]

That most people were poor prior to the Industrial Revolution was not due to an uneven distribution of income, but was due to the low level of output throughout the world. While rich people grew richer, a redistribution of income would not have alleviated the poverty of the masses.

Simply put, man was not able to raise his standard of living above the subsistence level. While some progress was made in some countries, the limited sources of energy—man's muscle, water, plants, and animals—prevented economic progress. The Industrial Revolution can be viewed as the initiation of a process which introduced large-scale exploitation of new sources of energy by means of inanimate devices.[95]

The limited energy available for production prior to industrialization and the history of a universally impoverished mankind spelled disaster for the black in the United States. Slavery was one consequence of the scarcity of other forms of energy; it was profitably instituted because other sources of energy were inadequate or too costly. The low level of production meant that most people would be poor, an economic fact of life that coincided with religious training. Furthermore, the "haves" had reason to keep the status quo by keeping the "have nots" in their place. If the poor improved their economic status, there was reason to believe they would replace some of the "haves" rather than increase the size of this rank. Slavery was an ideal way of keeping a large group of "have nots" in their place, a fact of life noted by Benjamin Franklin.

The year 1776 is noteworthy for at least two events. One of these is familiar to all Americans. The other is the publication of Adam Smith's *Wealth of Nations*.[96] Although there were antecedents, this book provided the foundation for "classical economics." Smith, along with Malthus, Ricardo, and others, developed a system of economic theory which came to dominate economic thought in England and the United States.

Classical economics represented a distinct break from previous theories of value. Ethical considerations had always played a major role in attempts to explain price and value.[97] Previously, economic theorists were concerned with the just price or the fair price; they were preoccupied with what the price should be. Classical economics, however, was positive rather than normative economics; it dealt with "what is" rather than with "what should be."

Classical economics provides the foundation for much of economic theory followed today. There have been changes, corrections, improvements, extensions, and clarifications, but the basic framework established by the classicists still provides the core for current micro theory. Neoclassical and modern economic thought will be discussed subsequently, but several aspects of classical economics should be noted at this point.

Adam Smith described an economic system in which a large number of buyers and sellers interacted in such a way that the general welfare was positively promoted. Every individual in this system freely pursued his own interests—indeed he must be acting selfishly—but the net result is a better society than one in which people consciously promote the "public interest." The interaction of a large number of buyers and sellers assured this result as if there were an "invisible hand" at work.

The rationale underlying this theory is essentially the same as that used in the United States today. Market competition, according to Smith, guarantees that producers will supply goods that consumers want at prices representing the worth of the goods (what it costs the person who brings it to market); the social value of the goods will be equal to the social cost of producing them. Additionally, competition guarantees efficient management, reducing costs of production to the lowest possible level. Therefore, a free market assures the production of goods wanted by society through the profit incentive, prices are controlled by competition, and efficiency in production is necessary to meet the price of the competitor.

Explicit in the Smithian system is, as everybody knows, a laissez-faire stand wherein the government was to remain neutral. Government was not to concern itself with short-run economic welfare or economic growth. Smith saw the state as a wasteful and extravagant institution which private industry could support if left alone. It is apparent that with Adam Smith and the *Wealth of Nations* we have a system of economic thought which shows little concern for those who cannot do well economically. It is a system which is more concerned with the harm government can do than with the plight of the unfortunate. The invisible hand and laissez-faire concepts do not help those on the lower end of income distribution. More than that, in discouraging state interference in economic affairs, the status quo, including slavery, is protected. Religion, at least, promised a hereafter while it saw little hope on earth.

Smith was by no means the only classical economist. Certainly the writings of Malthus, Ricardo, and others significantly affected nineteenth-century economic thought. While Smith optimistically viewed society's prospects for economic well being, Malthus gave classical economics a pessimistic outlook from which it never recovered.[98] He argued that population, increasing at a "geometric ratio," would, unless checked, outstrip the supply of food which grew at an "arithmetic ratio." Malthus feared that the population explosion could be checked only by economic misery. Improvement in the standard of living of workingmen leads to an increase in population, bringing the standard of living back down to a subsistence level.

23

Accordingly, most of mankind was doomed to perpetual poverty. This profoundly affected David Ricardo, who popularized Malthusian theory.

Ricardo gave classical economics its most consistent and systematic presentation; his explanation of production and distribution provided a fairly consistent economic theory. While taking the same general approach as Smith, Ricardo incorporated the pessimistic views of Malthus with respect to population and food production.[99]

The "Ricardian system" has four major propositions:

1. Population will expand whenever the wages paid to labor are above the subsistence level.

2. Increases in food production are subject to the law of diminishing returns in an expanding population. As more labor is used, the additional product decreases.

3. The rental value of land (the landlord's income) will equal the difference between the product by a given amount of labor on a piece of land and the product produced by the same amount of labor on the least fertile piece of land.

4. Capitalists accumulate capital only when the rate of return, or profit, is sufficiently attractive.[100]

These propositions can be put together to explain the entire economic system and the natural progress of society. While population is small, only the most fertile lands are used to produce foods. Therefore, rents are low and leftover income is shared between capitalist and worker in the form of profits and wages. Only the landlord is dissatisfied.

While profits are high, capitalists accumulate more capital and bid for more laborers. This raises wages above the subsistence level, and population expands. In turn, society must use more and poorer land to produce the necessary food, leading to diminishing returns and increased rents.

The process continues until the population grows so large and rent is so high that wages are driven downward to the subsistence level, and profits disappear so that capitalists are unwilling to accumulate more capital. This is the stationary state. Population will not increase while wages are at a subsistence level. Without profit and additional capital accumulation, wages cannot rise and progress is impossible unless external change takes place. Adam Smith had foreseen the possibility of this unpleasant state of affairs, but only as a distant prospect. For Ricardo, it was a current and very real possibility.

Classical economics was developed in a country without slavery and with virtually no blacks. If slavery had existed in England, perhaps Smith, Malthus, and Ricardo would have had something to say on the subject. As it was, the subject was ignored. This system of thought also is one which is based upon the ideas and problems of an agrarian economy. The con-

24

cern with land and highly competitive markets is less relevant as a country becomes industrialized.

Classical economics provided the nineteenth-century framework for politicians and leaders with a positive rather than normative theory, proclaiming that people are as well off as they can be and calling for a laissez-faire policy by the state since most people are doomed to live at the subsistence level. This philosophy is not likely to stimulate or encourage people and leaders to concern themselves with the black slave. The black certainly lived at the subsistence level or better, which was the lot of most of the white society. This economic philosophy shaped the political and legal thought of the day.

Slavery was not justified by the classical economist and, philosophically, each man was free to choose his way of life. The economic theorist did not specifically deal with slavery, and the political and philosophical implications were ignored. This type of economic theory did provide a convenient method of avoiding confrontation with an uncomfortable "noneconomic" issue. If government neutrality is desirable, then this also applies to the jurist who also ignored the impact of his decision upon the black.

It is perhaps noteworthy that classical economics developed when it did. Classical economics began and developed during the early and middle stages of the Industrial Revolution. It became popular at a time when many issues excluded from its framework were probably more relevant than ever before. For example, industrial technology and the relative standards of living of the rich and poor were ignored. The new technology doomed the small entrepreneur and paved the way for the large firm and concentration of industry, making some of the classical theory obsolete. Additionally, the abysmal standard of living of the working classes in England in these years is well documented. This line of reasoning can be pushed too far, but it may be fair to reason that classical theory was the work of apologists protecting the status quo.

The principal exponents of classical theory were from the middle and upper classes who needed religious and economic support to maintain their position. Classical economics, with the invisible hand assuring the optimum level of economic welfare, was the ideal rationalization for laissez-faire policy. The accumulation of wealth by a few and the unbelievable squalor in which the masses lived was rationalized. The Industrial Revolution introduced the possibility that universal poverty need not exist. However, the economic theory developed, rationalized, and facilitated the continuation of poverty for the "have nots." The parallel between this and the rationalization of slavery is clear.

Turning to economic conditions in the United States, one of the most powerful factors behind the existence and growth of slavery in the South was its profitability. While some dispute the profitability of slavery,[101] the most thorough and convincing study concludes that slavery was an economically viable and profitable institution in the South.[102]

The profitability of slavery in the South varied with the quality of the land.[103] Slaves in the fields returned a handsome profit where the land was rich. Where the quality of the soil was poor, raising and selling slaves to the owners of good land was profitable.

Profit from slavery could not be maintained, however, without expanding slave agriculture into the new territories. Continued and increased demand for slaves was necessary to keep slave raising profitable. Expansion into new territory was necessary to maintain profits from slave labor after cotton depleted the soil and to push the political power of the slaveholding states.

The economic gains derived from slavery caused Southern political and social leaders to do all they could to prevent any interference with slavery. The profit from cotton was also a significant factor in the drive to bring more slave states into the Union.

The need to maintain and expand slavery in order to continue and expand profits has had serious consequences which are still felt today. The economic development of the South before and after the Civil War lagged behind the rest of the nation. The reliance upon slave labor and the obsession with the black problem, which has dominated Southern political, social, and economic thought, has contributed substantially to the economic downfall in the South.

Prior to the Civil War, the North began to industrialize while the South continued to rely on King Cotton. The failure of the South to industrialize is not entirely attributable to the lack of capital or productive surplus which could be invested in industry. It may well be that the fundamental reason for the failure of industrial capitalism to develop in the South was slavery and all its consequences.[104] It prevented the development of elements necessary for a capitalistic society—dynamic markets, mobile labor force, the "entrepreneurial" mentality, etc. The slave system led to profits, but the price was the Southern obsession with the black, an obsession that led to the suppression of the type of social rationality typically associated with industrial capitalism.

The South did not develop the elements of a modern market economy. Large elements of its labor force were not paid wages and, thus, were isolated from the system of exchange; it did not have a mobile labor force. This prohibited the development of well-functioning markets for goods and labor. After 1820, it was basically a one-crop economy, where only a handful benefited from economic growth. Under such conditions, prosperity does

26

not push through all layers of society. Accordingly, the buyers necessary for mass production were not available in the South; nor were the markets for selling goods to large numbers able to develop. Most Southern effort was directed toward the rationalization of slavery, and economic development and capital accumulation were secondary.

The economic consequences of slavery for the black were several. The black slave was prevented from partaking in whatever economic progress there was. However, the long-run consequences were even more serious. He was denied the education and training needed to earn a decent wage when he was freed. Slavery and segregation have had serious effects upon the black's family life and lowered his incentive to attempt to succeed in a white-dominated world. Slavery and its effect upon southern thought also drastically curtailed the economic development of the South. Per capita income in the South was only 70 per cent of the national average in 1840; by 1930 it was only 55 per cent of the national average.[105] Southerners, especially blacks, continued to have a low standard of living. The slow economic development in this area meant fewer jobs and the black was seen as an economic threat by the poor white. To eliminate this threat, segregation was rigidly enforced, perpetuating the poverty of the black man.

Law and Politics to the Civil War

Colonial prejudice was visible almost as soon as the European made contact with the Indian and black. Besides being different, the Indian held land needed by the white. Protestantism did not condemn ambition; as indicated, acquisition was taken as a sign of the Lord's blessing. Knowing that religious leaders would not interfere, the Indian was easy prey for the white settler. Hatred is easily fanned when something is wanted that the other has. But dislike of the black by the European is more difficult to explain since the economic motive was initially absent; the colonial black was penniless and without property. The white initially categorized the black as a villein or vagrant; labor can be exploited without having to resort to slavery. Either the black was an economic threat, which hardly seems possible in a territory so vast, rich, and underpopulated, or his difference was enough to instill white hostility.

The first blacks to arrive in the colonies came in 1619; by 1630 the Virginia Assembly adopted a resolution calling for the whipping of white men and black women guilty of promiscuity—God could not be dishonored.[106] There was precedent under English law for punishing "heretical" mating. In 1222, a deacon was burned to death when he converted to Judaism because of his love of a Jewess.[107] This decision became authority, without legislative enactment, for burning the heretic. If a Christian-turned-Jew can be burned for marrying a Jewess, a black and a white spending a night together can be whipped in spite of the passage of 400 years.

Laws passed in the colonies placed the white on a separate footing from the black—the black was forbidden freedom of movement between colonies; firearms could not be carried; miscegenation laws were enacted; laws against "insurrection" were passed; education was forbidden; etc.[108] Congress approved delegates to a constitutional convention for Missouri elected by whites only; yet when Missouri was admitted to statehood in 1821, free blacks were constitutionally guaranteed the same "privileges and immunities" as whites. In 1847, Representative Wilmot of Pennsylvania sought to exclude slaves from territory acquired from Mexico so that the white would not live in fear of the black.[109] In 1828, the Senate Foreign Relations Committee tabled a proposal to colonize the free black who was needed to provide cheap and menial labor.[110]

The slave could not obtain or assign a patent because the law did not classify him as a person.[111] Congress in 1850 outlawed the harboring of an escaped slave, placing the burden of proof upon the black to establish that he was a freeman rather than the federal government proving that he was a slave. The Fugitive Slave Act of 1793 legalized slavery in the District of Columbia. The United States refused to recognize the black government of Haiti.

Lynch "law" in the South was supported by

> the overwhelming majority of the community, based as it was on the principle of self protection. . . . Its orderly procedures, its use of the democratic process of mass meeting and election of officers, its leadership drawn from the respected membership of the community . . . all combined to reduce any lingering doubts of its (lynch) legality and to allay any suspicions of mob law. . . .[112]

With such overwhelming approval from the good folk in the community, lynching took on the character of state-initiated justice. And the black was lynched.

There was almost unanimous agreement, similar to the church view previously cited, that the constitutional guarantee of freedom of speech did not protect the abolitionist.

Professor Beard holds that one reason the South supported the Constitution was white fear of the black. While there was unofficial national unity at the time of the Revolutionary War, the reason for cohesion ended when the proposed Constitution was debated. Membership in the new nation might prove economically disadvantageous, but fear of the black was sufficiently strong—and the fear had to be strong to risk economic injury—to lead to southern backing for a centralized government capable of supressing a black revolt.[113] Because state militias were weak and costly to maintain, the federal government would sponsor a military or police force sufficiently strong to protect our sovereignty against foreign aggression and prevent bloodshed in the South. In this way, states outlawing slavery would defray the cost of supporting the aristocratic planter in the South. Rather than risk the proposed amalgamation of states, northern leaders accepted slavery in the South as a condition for its support for a federated form of government.

There are historians who claim that Beard minimized the importance of slavery in his interpretation of constitutional history. Madison, for example, took note of the sharp division between slaveowning and nonslaveholding interests.[114]

Southern states, in exchange for supporting the Constitution, were permitted, in Article I, Section 9, to import slaves for twenty years and escaped slaves could even be followed to a state outlawing slavery.[115] Although the South looked upon the black as a chattel or an appendage to real property, another concession, in Article I, Section 2, granted to the slave state was that three-fifths of a black was added to its population count, leading to increased representation in the House of Representatives. Article IV, Section 2, called for the return of fugitive slaves from states where slavery was not practiced.

The Constitution is evidence of a bargain between the North and the South: how can there be liberty, equality, pursuit of happiness, and slavery? By allowing representation in the House to be geared to slavery, by permitting the importation of slaves until 1808 even though Congress had the power to regulate interstate commerce, by permitting the capture of fugitive slaves in the nonslave states, drafters of the Constitution put themselves on the side of slavery. Equality in the United States was a myth at the inception.

Blacks were enlisted in the Continental Army to prevent them from joining the British Army.[116]

Jefferson prior to and after the Revolutionary War favored the abolition of slavery, feeling that most whites favored this. Prior to the Revolutionary War, ending slavery was difficult because England did not want to lose this profitable trade.[117] But the Declaration of Independence was adopted without outlawing slavery, in spite of the sentiment expressed that "all men are created equal." Although "all men are created equal" is a color blind expression which could lead to a political stand outlawing slavery, it can be reasoned that slavery was not expressly prohibited or otherwise declared illegal, or that the federal government was to remain neutral, leaving the decision to the state. It must be remembered that Jefferson

29

represented the aristocratic farmer, whose wealth was tied to slavehold-ing.[118]

That representatives from northern states capitulated so completely to southern will to assure national unity requires additional explanation. Some historians overemphasize and eulogize the moral spirit engulfing the colonies at the time of the Revolutionary War. Commercial interests, and not the run-of-the-mill colonial, benefited most by tax relief; and freedom from English rule could have been secondary to the "buck." Colonial leaders were landowners and merchants; in fact, most of the military came from the bourgeois. If the Revolutionary War is viewed as an economic war, the framers of the Declaration of Independence did not intend to include the black in the concept that "all men are created equal."[119] The black slave to the economic man represented an investment.

Some Southern support for the Constitution was based upon a rationale that proved untrue. Southern leaders felt that the bulk of the population in the United States would ultimately live in the South so that they would control Congress.[120]

Some political leaders argued that ending slavery would set a precedent which would permit government tampering with all private property.

In summation, legislators and jurists, reflecting popular will, treated the black as personal property. This position dovetailed with the economics of the plantation and the prominent religions. Whereas the important wealth before the Industrial Revolution was represented by real property, the large planter frequently had an even larger investment in the slave.[121] When Fort Sumter erupted, four million slaves and 250,000 black freemen lived in the South.[122]

Contrary to the magnolia-like look, such as in "Gone With the Wind," where the slave is pictured laboring contentedly and loved, evidence points to a strong desire for freedom. Slaves brought to the states frequently killed themselves and sought to inflict serious injury upon their masters. A black rebellion is recorded as early as 1663.[123]

The influence of Thomas Paine and Benjamin Franklin, who felt that freedom was a natural right due all men, led to the freeing of 20,000 slaves by 1800. The Virginia Constitution prior to the Civil War, to protect its white citizens, provided that emancipated blacks must leave within twelve months or return to slavery.[124] In South Carolina, blacks outnumbered whites; an important factor underlying the prohibition against importing more slaves into the United States was the fear of the numerical increase of the black.

Legislatively contained, particularly after mass uprisings, and his lack of standing in the courtroom, the black had nowhere to turn for help; his only protection in court hinged upon his value to the owner.

The approach and rationalization of legislators and jurists dedicated to laissez faire is interesting. If the black is a chattel, economic theory calls for complete control by the owner, and government agencies are to remain neutral. Conceptually, the plantation owner will take care of his property, which in the long run benefits society. But many laws were passed to help the slave trader, presumably because of public interest. As an observation, laissez faire is resorted to or sought where government interference is not wanted; seldom is laissez faire preached when the helping hand of the government is wanted. While conceding the advantages of laissez faire, complete abdication by government to industry is intolerable.

To "balance the budget," if laws are passed to aid the slaveowner, laws should be passed to prevent mistreatment of the slave. Laws were passed to keep the black in slavery, laws which were on the whole stringently enforced; but laws designed to protect the black were seldom passed or invoked. Rarely was a slaveowner convicted of mistreating a slave.[125] In fact, court rules prevented the black from testifying against the white.

Not until 1800 was slavery seriously challenged.[126] In fact, Garrison, a leading abolitionist, felt that his stand against slavery was unpopular in the North. Because he favored the demise of slavery, Garrison was charged with being antireligious.[127]

The following reasons were advanced against outlawing slavery:

1. Blacks would move North if slavery ended.
2. The South would economically boycott the North if abolition were pressed.
3. Only the educated and wealthy were entitled to freedom.
4. The white would be unsafe if the black were freed.
5. The purity of "Teutonic" blood must be maintained.
6. The abolitionist and black, if freed, would form an alliance to control the federal government, ultimately leading to its destruction.
7. Black and white would compete for jobs, leading to the reduction of wages.
8. The entire economic system in the South would be destroyed.
9. There is little difference between slave and free labor: it was simply an exchange of one master for another. In fact, some reasoned that the black slave was better treated than the white freeman who did not represent an investment and was easily replaced.

Of the rationale presented to support slavery, only two carry substance. That the safety of the white would be endangered if the black were freed is realistic. An ex-slave will resent his captor, especially if ill-treated, and grudges will be harbored. Nevertheless, white fear of the black, much of it based upon uprisings occurring in the past, bordered upon the hysterical. That the economic system so conservatively and ill-advisedly built up in the South would crumble was a foregone conclusion, and competition for jobs between black and white was bound to be keen until industry developed.

Some viewed the slaveholding dispute as an economic battle between northern capital and agrarian interests in the South; additionally a battle for political power.[128] During the Civil War, northern businessmen profited by selling goods to the Army; the end of Civil War left Northerners with an abundance of capital and sufficient political influence to reap further economic reward ushered in by the Industrial Revolution.

The North was more receptive to economic change than the South; and northern capitalists, aware of changes taking place in England, were ready to move. The North favored tariffs, homestead laws, national banking, etc., all opposed by influential southern leaders. Leaders of the Republican Party promoted a policy of laissez faire toward industry while, at the same time, approving considerable financial aid to railroads and others.

The action and stand taken by important public figures toward the black prior to the Civil War is illuminating. Jefferson kept slaves while condemning slavery: slaves were sold to pay his debts, Monticello was built with slave labor, and his slaves were not given their freedom upon his death.[129] Yet Jefferson condemned King George for supporting the slavers, a violation of the natural rights of man.[130] Jefferson also felt that the black, even if freed, could not be assimilated in the United States. Both Jefferson and Washington, and later Lincoln, favored sending the black elsewhere. Benjamin Franklin, while against slavery, did not favor bringing the black to this continent.[131]

Whatever his moral commitment, Lincoln never considered the black an equal of the white. Lincoln refused to sign a petition to change the law in Illinois barring blacks from testifying against whites in court.[132] Lincoln's candidacy on the Republican Party ticket was based on his reputation as a middle-of-the-roader, neither favoring abolition nor the spread of slavery to the territories. Abolitionists felt that the Republican Party handicapped the push to end slavery because it was only against the further spread of slavery. Lincoln, upon assuming the presidency, resisted the spread of slavery, which limited the political power of the South and led to a fear that slavery would disappear unless moved into the western territories.[133]

In 1858, Lincoln said:

> . . . I am not, nor ever have been, in favor of bringing about in any way the social and political equality of the black and white races—that I am not nor ever have been in favor of making voters or jurors of negroes, nor of qualifying them to hold office, nor to intermarry with white people, and I will say in addition to this that there is a physical difference between the black and white races. . . . And . . . while they do remain together there

must be the position of superior and inferior, and I as much as any other man am in favor of having the superior position assigned to the white race.[134]

Lincoln advocated the gradual elimination of slavery, compensating the slaveowner for his loss and colonizing the black elsewhere.[135] Some members of Congress and Republican Party standard bearers felt that Lincoln, during his first term in office, had not acted vigorously enough to help the slave.[136] Lincoln, prior to his election, said,

> If all earthly powers were given to me, I should not know what to do, as to the existing institution. My first impulse would be to free all the slaves, and send them to Liberia. . . . But (this) is impossible. . . . Free them, and make them politically and socially, our equals? My own feelings will not admit of this; and if mine would, we well know that those of the great mass of white people will not.[137]

In 1862, General Hunter proclaimed martial law along the coast line of South Carolina, Georgia, and Florida, and issued an order emancipating all slaves, which was rescinded by Lincoln.[138] In the same year, Lincoln negotiated a contract with a promoter to colonize more than 450 freed slaves in Haiti.[139]

In 1861, Secretary of War Cameron said the military establishment did not want colored troops. Congress, on July 17, 1862, did pass two bills authorizing the use of black soldiers. But Lincoln was slow to use black troops because he did not want to offend Kentucky.[140]

During the Civil War, General Sherman balked at using black soldiers. In fact, General Grant may have been reluctant to use black troops. Black soldiers captured during the war by the South were poorly treated when compared to treatment accorded white captives.[141]

Another indicator of how unfairly the cards had been stacked against the black is the university community. In southern colleges and universities, slavery as a topic of discussion was banned. One seminary expelled students who openly condemned slavery. And this approach was common in the North. Students at Amherst could not discuss slavery in the classroom. Western Reserve College pressured its faculty to drop its public stand favoring abolition.[142]

CHAPTER FOUR ✂ THE AFTERMATH

Having fought a successful war, northern leaders in the executive, legislative, and judicial branches of government were in a position to aid the ex-slave in the South. Skeleton policy would have to be formulated to provide for feeding, educating, and training the black to take his place in a society in which industry would replace agriculture as the dominant economic force. While essentials were provided, the black would need protection to slowly inch his way into the white world. It was necessary that the black make immediate political progress to prevent unfair domination by the white, while the economic progress of the black was bound to be slower. Without a friend of substance or influence and with white fear of the black, the ex-slave lacking education and industrial know-how would need considerable help for a long time.

Religious leaders refused to challenge business interests or participate in politics, giving open support to white supremacy by remaining silent (what in law is called neutrality and in economics laissez faire). There is little evidence to indicate that religion was interested or could stomach the battle necessary to protect and promote the black. Industrial leaders in turn looked upon the occasional critic from the ministry as an interloper who should tend to church affairs. Industry was off and running after the Civil War, characterized by tremendous energy, ruthlessness, and an unwillingness to brook interference from the private or government critics. This was the age of expansion, by whatever means, in oil, railroads, manufacturing, etc., and there is considerable evidence that economic muscle was synonymous with political power.

To understand the black catastrophe after the Civil War, it is necessary to "feel the pulse" of those in a position to help the black. In this chapter, the role played by the economist, political leader, and jurist will be examined to show how the black was boxed in.

Economics: 1860 to 1930

Economic thought in the last half of the nineteenth century continued along the path established by the classicists in most respects. The policy prescription of laissez faire and the narrowing of the scope of economic theory continued. The group of people who could be called professional economists grew in number both in Europe and the United States, but the types of problems considered by the majority of them became increasingly specialized and, accordingly, of less concern to the noneconomist.

Karl Marx and his followers can be cited as the most obvious exceptions to this assertion, but Marx had little impact on the mainstream of economic thought in England or the United States. In fact, Marxist thought, especially in the United States, stimulated the defense of existing institutions against his criticisms.

Despite the continuity with earlier economics, there were some differences. Laissez faire was generally accepted, but not uncritically. The increasing professionalization of economics brought a change in tone, leading to a greater separation between ideology and analysis. Economists in the late nineteenth century could disagree about politics, but still be in substantial agreement about economic theory. Also, the future was viewed more optimistically. Economic conditions in industrialized countries improved substantially for the majority of the populace, and there was less reason to criticize the system; most effort was directed toward a close examination of how and why it worked as it did.

Almost all of the significant developments in economic thought during this period came from Europe (Mill, Jevons, Walras, and Marshall—all Europeans—all well known to anyone with even a casual acquaintance with the history of economic thought). They added greatly to the development of economic theory, refining, correcting, and enriching classical thought. However, the basic concepts relating to markets and competition were left unchanged. Free competition and laissez faire still received the blessings of the high priests of the economic profession as the means best suited to enrich society materially.

When a formal definition of optimal economic conditions was finally handed down and accepted by economists, society paid a price. All questions of interpersonal comparison or income distribution were omitted from consideration in defining the optimal economic state. In the name of science or objectivity, crucial economic questions were pushed aside and ignored by the mainstream of economic thinkers. These omissions include the problem of slavery and the economic status of the black. It is not surprising that European economic thought did not touch upon these problems because they were not relevant to the European situation, but American economists also ignored them, apparently because they were not interested in such problems or because they were not considered appropriate subjects for economic analysis.

One of the suppositions of traditional economic theory is that people are paid in accordance with their productivity, or, more exactly, the wage rate is equal to the marginal productivity of labor. This means that the wage rate for a particular skill in a particular market is determined by the productivity of the last unit of labor (with that skill) hired. The problem in uncritically accepting this as a prescription is that some people have very low productivity, and frequently the supply of such people is very large. This means their wages will be very low. This was especially true of blacks after the Civil War, and their opportunities for developing adequate skills were virtually nonexistent or even illegal. Reliance upon market-determined wages did not hurt whites nearly as much, because they generally had higher skills and much more opportunity to improve upon their existing skills. Another problem was that employers for noneconomic reasons refused to hire blacks even when they were blessed with the requisite skill, dooming blacks to low incomes. However, many economists blithely accepted the beneficence of the invisible hand and accepted the prescription of laissez faire.

A number of Supreme Court decisions during this period seemed to accept this approach. Many laws which "interfered" with business operations, such as child and woman labor laws and minimum wage laws, were declared unconstitutional.[143]

Behind the doctrine of laissez faire was an economic theory based on beneficence of the invisible hand, a theory based on the assumptions of perfect competition, knowledge of opportunities, perfect mobility of labor and other factors of production, and the rational behavior of consumers and producers. These assumptions have never been realistic for any economy, but some of them are especially unrealistic when applied to the postbellum South. Rational economic behavior and perfect labor mobility were notable by their absence. The black man was not included in the economy of the South in the manner assumed by this theory, and he suffered greatly because of this.

Economics had become an institutionalized discipline in the United States by the latter half of the nineteenth century; there were numerous professional economists, a few of whom enjoyed international reputations. Despite close ties with Europe and increasing sterilization of economic theory, some economists, notably Henry George and Thorsten Veblen, do not fit into this pattern.

Among those economists in the United States more conventional than George or Veblen, there was, nonetheless, a closer tie with social and political problems than in England. Despite the sterility of formal economics, many American economists did write on current real world economic problems. However, the black was not an economic link which received much attention.

Volume III of Joseph Dorfman's *The Economic Mind in American Civilization* has 470 pages on the period from 1860-1920.[144] Hundreds of economists and scores of issues are discussed in this volume, but the status of the black is never raised. Few people of consequence were interested in black welfare and economists were no exception. Furthermore, formal economic theory was not suitable for discussing this problem. And there was insufficient public concern with black welfare to engage the interest of economists willing to go beyond the confines of formal economic theory.

The Political Arena

Political leaders in the North knew that the black would need considerable help to make the transition from slavery to freedom meaningful. Frederick Douglass, an ex-slave and leader in the black community, warned the public that the black would require extensive help and understanding.[145] Many abolitionists realized that political franchise and a basic education would not lead to equality of power between black and white without economic muscle.[146] During wartime, black soldiers were paid less than white soldiers. In the North, blacks by 1831 lived in segregated slums, were denied education, were segregated in the church, and were confined to menial jobs.[147] In the South, blacks were paid less than whites for the same work or not paid at all. When Lincoln pardoned the confederate soldiers after the Civil War on condition that they agree to uphold the Constitution, he doomed the black by promising the southern states that they could continue to control education and welfare programs.

The agency established in 1865 to aid the black was the Freedmen's Bureau, an adjunct of the War Department.[148] The most urgent need of the black was food and a rudimentary education, which the Bureau undertook to supply. More than 90 per cent of the blacks freed after the Civil War could not read or write.[149] To meet the emergency, blacks were quartered and fed on plantations taken over by the Army, surroundings associated with past injustice. Many of the Army overseers assigned to the Freedmen's Bureau could not appreciate the black revulsion against working in this environment.

Since agriculture was, for all practical purposes, the sole source of employment, and failing to sense the substantial economic change to come, the Bureau pushed the black into the fields. The Bureau leased to blacks forty acres of land formerly belonging to confederate soldiers with an understanding that title could be purchased in three years. But President Johnson granted amnesty to the southern planters and family estates were reclaimed.[150] Settling the black on a southern farm could have eased the economic burden for some, but it seems unlikely that this solution would have helped many. If land ownership was desirable, the federal government, the Bureau specifically, should have settled the black in territories where large farms could have been carved and rich soil was available; the

37

southern soil had already been depleted by the planting of cotton. Unfortunately, the western land was being held for the white settler.

Some blacks tried homesteading, but feeding a family and providing shelter proved an insurmountable burden.[151] The Bureau did serve as a clearinghouse for jobs and sponsored a training program for orphans and destitute children, sending them to foster homes to serve as apprentices.[152] This limited form of apprentice training was not meaningful because few homes in which he could learn a trade were open to the black child.

The Freedmen's Bureau was never able to meet the challenge with a full head of steam. General Howard, who presided over the Bureau, operated with too small a budget to help the black adequately. For example, although five million dollars was spent educating blacks, with 250,000 attending classes, it was a drop in the bucket when viewed from the perspective of black need.[153] Not only was the appropriation inadequate, but the typical white southerner was against education for the black who then would be unwilling to play a subservient role.[154] Forced to use Army personnel, whose salaries would be paid by the Army rather than the Bureau, General Howard, short of money, could not hire a sufficient number of civilians.[155] In fact, even the limited funding made available was not forthcoming until one year after the Bureau was in operation, an indication of how ready Congress was to help the black. Further hampering effective operation was the unwillingness of the South to cooperate with the Bureau, viewed as an adjunct of a conquering army and an occupation force. In addition, there was inefficiency within the Bureau.[156]

Because of an overabundance of cheap labor, scarcity of jobs, and need to protect the black, there was sentiment favoring the declaration of a minimum wage by the Freedmen's Bureau.[157] Nevertheless, General Howard refused to place a bottom on wages, following a laissez-faire philosophy because of variances in local conditions. The only guideline suggested by General Howard was that the blacks receive the same pay as their former owners received who allowed blacks to work temporarily for others. The Bureau did draw employment contracts to protect the black, but the planter was promised faithful performance, a display of proper respect, etc.[158] With Bureau approval, planters could withhold 50 per cent of the stipulated wage until the cotton season ended, and a field hand resigning prematurely would forfeit his unpaid wage. Gradually, the Freedmen's Bureau turned to the sharecropping agreement, which entitled the black to 50 per cent of the sale price of the crop to relieve the employer of supervising field hands.

With due respect to the economic, political, and legal theoreticians preaching self-help, the ex-slave could not make the economic and social transition without extensive and determined help. Society must accept full

38

responsibility for slavery and its aftermath and recognize the incalculable damage inflicted upon the black. It is our contention that with proper governmental programming after the Civil War, the black and white dilemma would be less grave today. As previously noted, Lincoln advocated the government purchase of slaves as the best means of ending slavery. If an owner can be compensated for the loss of his human property, then government can bear the cost of rekindling and retooling the black spirit. There is a willingness in economics and law to compensate a property owner for his loss but there is an unwillingness to rectify, financially, moral wrong.

The Civil War was costly, representing a huge outlay of public funds. The Civil War can be viewed as a conditioning process, preparing society mentally for the need to make large expenditures in the future. If spending conditioning did take place, it did not apply to the black. Society, it seems, is better prepared to spend money for war than to help citizens. As proof of this point, President Johnson vetoed a bill extending the life of the Freedmen's Bureau.[159]

Even with limited help—perhaps more accurately in spite of limited help —the black made some economic headway after the Civil War.[160] The black was counted as a complete person after the Civil War for the purpose of political representation. Political muscle leads to economic opportunity and the black made political progress. Blacks permitted to vote could push blacks into public office or demand concessions for their support. For example, in Louisiana, 103,334 blacks registered as voters in 1896.[161] An ex-slave represented Mississippi in the United States Senate. Louisiana elected a black governor while black lieutenant governors held office in Mississippi and South Carolina. A black sat on the Supreme Court in South Carolina. Black superintendents of education, state treasurers, adjutant generals, judges, and other state officials held office with regularity.[162]

The white South quickly outmaneuvered the black in politics and all gains were lost.[163] Alabama and South Carolina passed laws forbidding blacks to operate taverns or sell hard liquor. South Carolina forbade partnerships of white and black, and blacks could not practice a trade unless able to prove that they served an apprenticeship. Mississippi forbade black ownership of land except in cities sanctioning it.[164] Mississippi passed laws forbidding the rental of property to a black other than in an incorporated town. In Louisiana, blacks in certain parishes could not freely move about during the night unless a special permit was issued and they were in the employ of a white person.[165] With the economic depression beginning in 1870 and continuing during the 1880s and 1890s, the South was paralyzed. The black would have faced considerable economic difficulty even if an honest attempt were made to help him.

While southern leaders concentrated on the maintenance of political supremacy, northern businessmen took advantage of the agrarian conservatism in the South and forged ahead industrially. Both Lincoln and Johnson permitted southern leaders to participate in the policy decisions affecting the reconstruction of the South, assuring white supremacy. But the black was also important to the northern industrialist worshipping cheap labor and, if need be, union-busting labor. This businessman was the rational decision-maker worshipped by the economist and jurist. The era of the Robber Barons—characterized by ruthlessness and exploitation—was a period in which the accumulation of wealth was treated as God's will. The black could expect no understanding or mercy from political leaders in the South and northern industry.

White labor in the South knew that a living wage could not be earned farming, a point of view endorsed by the landowner. To remain a farm hand meant that the white worker was no better than the black. While the black could be exploited without criticism, the farmer could not treat the white similarly. As industry slowly opened in the South, the white took the newly created jobs and shut out the black. Where the black historically filled better jobs in industry, as in construction, he was quickly eliminated. By 1891, blacks only held 7,500 jobs in southern industry.[166] As industry and the demand for labor expanded, the black fell heir to the less desirable and poorer paying jobs.

Political leaders throughout the United States endorsed a policy calling for white dominance over the black. President Johnson distrusted the northern industrialist, feeling that government should be controlled by the small farmer—he did not envision the sharing of political and economic power with the black.[167] While against slavery, Johnson opposed the aristocratic and large farmer rather than sympathizing with the black. Johnson said, "Damn the negroes . . . I am fighting these traitorous aristocrats, their masters."[168] Johnson, to maximize the power of the small white farmer, would naturally push a state rights policy that was bound to keep the black shackled.[169]

The political compromise negotiated in 1876 restored white supremacy in the South. Leading Republicans would not oppose the election of Democrats to state office in Florida, Louisiana, and South Carolina (federal troops would also be withdrawn) while Hayes would be given the presidency which Tilden had won.[170]

Rutherford B. Hayes offered a scholarship to W. E. B. DuBois to study in Germany only after being assured that he was part white.[171] President Taft felt that the progress of the ex-slave was satisfactory, but that the race problem could be solved if the black, who was only suited for farming, would be relocated.[172] Teddy Roosevelt considered the black inferior and a coward. At the Republican Convention at which he was nominated for the presidency, he approved the decision refusing to seat a black delegation and disapproved of a civil rights platform.[173] Mr. Roosevelt discharged an entire battalion of blacks without a hearing after a riot in Texas.[174] Grover Cleveland approved of a speech made by Booker T. Washington which, in essence, called for segregation. President McKinley sat back while one southern state after another disenfranchised the black.

Campaigning for the presidency, Woodrow Wilson said that he would help the black to secure justice. Twenty orders were presented during the administration of Mr. Wilson calling for segregated transportation in the District of Columbia, restricting blacks to the enlisted rank in the military, and halting all black immigration.[175] By executive order, eating and toilet facilities provided for civil service workers were segregated. Postal and Treasury officials working in the South were authorized by Mr. Wilson to discharge or downgrade black employees. Thirty-five blacks in Atlanta were turned out of their jobs at the Post Office.[176] President Wilson stated that segregation was best for both races: he never appointed a black to hold public office in the South.[177]

The prejudice recorded—and more can be added—spotlights the implications of the Supreme Court position toward the black after the Civil War.

The Judicial Sphere

The Supreme Court reflected the prevailing attitude of the day in decisions touching upon the economic and political well-being of the black. While these decisions are sugar coated in the legal frill common to the period, the Supreme Court, just like the clergy, could not claim moral leadership.[178] While the Supreme Court, as some claim, may not be constituted to provide moral leadership, it can move in to stop injustice. The decisions, however, reflect hostility to the black and a lack of concern for his treatment.

The Thirteenth Amendment was designed by Congress to be used offensively, permitting the enactment of legislation to prevent "involuntary servitude."[179] The Executive Proclamation issued by Mr. Lincoln on January 1, 1863, ending slavery, applied to all confederate states except parts of Louisiana, Virginia, and Tennessee. The Thirteenth Amendment was necessary to counteract the Black Codes passed in the southern states and to outlaw slavery in Louisiana, Virginia, and Tennessee. Not only was the state told that the black could not be treated unfairly, but the same admonition was hurled at the private citizen.

The Senate approved the Thirteenth Amendment on April 4, 1864, but it was not approved by the House of Representatives. After Lincoln was re-elected in 1864, a sufficient number of House Democrats changed their vote or abstained from voting so that the Thirteenth Amendment was ap-

41

proved. In 1865, three-fourths of the states approved the Thirteenth Amendment.[180]

The Fourteenth Amendment was another matter. The protections specified and the broad idealistic terminology could have helped the black cause considerably. However, two limitations in the Fourteenth Amendment confine its reach, creating, if you will, exceptions to the idealism expressed. By opening the Fourteenth Amendment with a warning to the state only, private discrimination, however injurious to the black, could continue unchecked. Where discrimination is the rule and not the exception, prohibiting state discrimination only is not going to help those oppressed. Second, while the Thirteenth Amendment authorized Congress to enact legislation preventing "involuntary servitude," the Fourteenth Amendment permitted the passage of federal legislation *after* state hostility was exhibited against the black. The Fourteenth Amendment provided defensive support, a rear guard protection for the benefit of the black. The ex-slave unquestionably needed protection from executive, legislative, and judicial hostility at a state level, but, in addition, his well-being needed positive promotion and protection from private discrimination. Private and public hostility was overwhelming and, as previously maintained, political and private economic power is inseparable. A question worthy of exploration is whether there is public hostility when a state ignores pronounced patterns of private discrimination against the black. For example, the lynchings and violence directed against the black in the South could not have reached such proportions unless public officials turned their backs. The black in the South was completely disenfranchised, in spite of the Fifteenth Amendment, with government participation. And let there be no misunderstanding—the Thirteenth and Fourteenth Amendments were intentional intrusions upon state rights. Since the intrusions were intentional, the unwillingness of jurists to interfere with state "prerogatives" is somewhat strange. This judicial restraint spelled doom for the black desperately in need of federal help. Since more than 90 per cent of the black population resided in the South and the southern states were determined to keep the black "in place," a limited construction of federal power was tantamount to throwing the black to the lions.

There is a distinct difference between the congressional authorizations in the Thirteenth and Fourteenth Amendments, which leads to interpretative distinctions. The offensive authorization in the Thirteenth Amendment permits long-range planning by government as well as the correction of immediate wrong, while the defensive authorization of the Fourteenth Amendment permits only the correction of past and immediate wrong. That discrimination can take on many forms needs little amplification, and the congressional correction of one wrong under the Fourteenth Amendment leads to a state search for other methods. Since each situation is different, justice is delayed and the black frustrated. Without doubt, the South, with northern consent, found many ingenious methods to delay black progress.

The offensive action permitted under the Thirteenth Amendment could hardly result in meaningful promotion of black welfare since it condemns only "involuntary servitude." Unless uniquely interpreted, the reach of the Thirteenth Amendment was destined to be minimal, a fact known to political leaders. In contrast, the Fourteenth Amendment with its wide reach could support a wide program of promotional legislation. By including safety valves in the total package—the prohibition against affirmative action by Congress and allowing only the correction of state action—the usefulness of the Fourteenth Amendment was limited. In any event it would have been difficult for Congress to turn down the Thirteenth Amendment when a war had been fought to end slavery. But the Fourteenth Amendment was another matter—neither Congress nor society was ready to let the black move upward.

In *Jones v. Alfred H. Mayer Co.*,[181] the Supreme Court in 1968 held that a black was illegally denied the right to purchase a home in a new development and Section 2 of the Civil Rights Act of 1866 was clearly violated. Section 2 provides that "(a)ll citizens . . . shall have the . . . right . . . to inherit, purchase, lease, sell, hold, and convey real and personal property." Interestingly, the Supreme Court held that the constitutional support for Section 2 was the Thirteenth Amendment, and that to deny the black the right to buy a home was a remnant of his status as a slave. In the *Civil Rights Cases*, subsequently discussed, the Supreme Court was unwilling to find a violation of the Thirteenth Amendment when blacks were not permitted the temporary use of privately owned facilities. While differences can be pointed to between *Jones* and the *Civil Rights Cases*, the most significant difference appears to be the changing philosophy of the Supreme Court.

There is some evidence that the Civil War Amendments were illegally adopted.[182] Members of Congress rebelled against supporting the Thirteenth Amendment, pointing to the holy of holies, the desirability of state regulation. The Thirteenth Amendment did not call for black and white equality, and the preservation of state rights is a rallying point around which the prohibition against "involuntary servitude" can be ignored. While the federal government did assume responsibility for guarding against conditions approximating "involuntary servitude," the Thirteenth Amendment did nothing (until 1968) to cushion the inevitable black pain of entering the white world.[183]

The Fourteenth Amendment may have been pushed politically to back the creation of the Freedmen's Bureau; there was some question whether

43

the Thirteenth Amendment could be used as the constitutional crutch for the exercise of federal power.[184] But the privileges and immunities, equal protection and due process provisions of the Fourteenth Amendment go beyond the support of the Freedmen's Bureau and a weak signal was sent to those believing in equality that the black was to be included in the concept of "all men are equal."

In the *Civil Rights Cases*[185] the Supreme Court followed with precision the language of the Fourteenth Amendment, ruling that public discrimination was forbidden and private discrimination constitutionally untouched. The *Civil Rights Cases* has undergone considerable dissection, and those disagreeing with the majority decision point to the dissenting opinion by Justice Harlan, who found state action because private institutions, like hotelkeepers and railroads, operate under special rules and government privileges. Rather than rehash the pros and cons of the majority decision in the *Civil Rights Cases*, a more worthwhile pursuit is the exploration of its meaning to the black.

The most damaging aspect to the black of the decision in the *Civil Rights Cases* was the clear signal to employers that the federal government would not stop private discrimination. To fully appreciate the impact of this decision, the Thirteenth and Fourteenth Amendments and the *Civil Rights Cases* decision came at a time when racial and religious discrimination was flagrant. The Civil War resulted in the suspension of southern hostility toward the Catholic Church, but it was resumed, to a lesser degree, thereafter.[186] During and after the Civil War, Mormons practicing polygamy faced intense hostility. Antisemitism increased after the Civil War.[187] Although prohibited by state law, the testimony of a black helped to convict Leo Frank, a Jew, for killing a girl in Marietta, Georgia. Congress showed interest in the land held by some Indian tribes and steps were taken to "integrate" them; Indians at this point were considered fit for integration while blacks were best segregated.

Chinese immigrating to California were free men.[188] When needed to build railroads and work in mines, Orientals were considered hard workers and good citizens. As economic conditions changed and the supply of labor increased, the Chinese, by popular acclaim, turned into poor citizens. Many criminal acts were perpetrated by white citizens against the Chinese. Much of the ill-will directed against Orientals came from southerners immigrating to California. Northern legislators supported the anti-Chinese policy after blacks moved to the northern cities. This prejudice culminated in legislation when southern and western legislators cooperated to pass the Chinese Exclusion Act of 1882 and citizenship was denied to Orientals. In light of the insistence by the federal government that American visitation and movement in China be unrestricted—troops were sent to China to protect American citizens during the Boxer Rebellion—it is strange that the Chinese in California were not protected. Political leaders in the United States, believing in state rights, would not appreciate the absence of a strong centralized government in Peking when protection was demanded for American citizens in China. The Chinese government insisted that protection be given to Orientals in the United States, to which the State Department responded that the federal government could not interfere with state jurisdiction. When Japanese, Mexican, and Puerto Rican people came to the United States, they were given the same treatment as the Chinese.[189] With discrimination rampant, the ex-slave could not expect fair treatment.

It is claimed that the black did not progress because of a lack of drive and education while Orientals were accused of having too much drive. The Jew was considered too pushy, acquisitive, and tricky.

To further illustrate the damage caused by limiting the reach of the Fourteenth Amendment, an entire generation of black leaders in the South were killed or discouraged by physical violence between 1877 and 1880.[190] Lynchings in the South increased after 1882 when whites began to put down black "agitators."[191] One author states:

> To read the details of lynching is to be reminded of the torture of the Middle Ages. . . . The victims were lucky indeed if they were . . . hanged. In Paris, Texas, in 1893 a Negro had his eyes gouged out with a red-hot poker before he was burned to death. In Arkansas . . . a crowd of five hundred . . . watched a Negro slowly burned to death. He was chained to a log and "fairly cooked to death" as small piles of damp leaves were burned under different parts of his body. When the victim would try to hasten his own death by swallowing hot ashes, his tormentors would kick the ashes out of his reach. . . . A reporter from the Memphis Press . . . noted how after the victim was dead there was a wild scramble of the mob to secure his bones as souvenirs. W. E. B. Du Bois tells of seeing the fingers of a lynched Negro displayed . . . in Atlanta. Sometimes victims had their teeth pulled out one by one, their fingers and toes chopped off by axes while they were still alive, and frequently they were castrated or otherwise mutilated. . . .[192]

Many of the lynchings must be considered state sanctioned—public officials did nothing to stop them.[193]

State rights is a constitutional and legal concept that has played an important role in the United States. If this philosophy is pushed to perpetuate a caste system, there is some evidence of state action violating the Fourteenth Amendment. When taking its stand in the *Civil Rights Cases*, the Supreme Court was aware of what was going on in the South. The decision in the *Civil Rights Cases* pushes, and not too gently, state authority to do what it will. Was there federal action violating the Fifth Amendment when

45

the Supreme Court justices in the *Civil Rights Cases* knowingly permitted the continued abuse of the black while promoting state rights? Some Supreme Court justices deciding the *Civil Rights Cases* did not feel that the mushrooming federal power was desirable.[194]

That the concept of state rights was pushed by the South to better control the black is irrefutable; probably the most notorious use of the doctrine of state rights is the maintenance of white supremacy. In Mississippi, blacks were beaten to extract a confession to a crime. The Mississippi Attorney General defended the police by claiming state rights, while the Mississippi Supreme Court nodded its approval.[195] Constitutional and legal doctrine prevailing at the time of the *Civil Rights Cases* shows a greater preoccupation with state rights than today and the Supreme Court attitude must be weighed in this light. The growth of the concept of interstate commerce doomed much of the political theory favoring state rights.[196]

Furthermore, the Supreme Court, in keeping with the prevailing economic theory of the day, promoted industry, downgrading the importance of unions and minority and individual rights. The federal government maintained a position of neutrality toward industry on the theory that this would promote the well-being of society. But how would a hands-off policy help the black, knowing that the private sector of the economy consistently discriminated against him?

The state rights doctrine could have been judicially developed while protecting the black at the same time. As a minimum, the Fourteenth Amendment could have been interpreted to prohibit state action and inaction grossly injurious to the black. Actually, the equal protection clause of the Fourteenth Amendment limits the promotion of state rights. The state government which fails to protect all citizens equally does not fulfill its constitutional obligation to provide equal protection.[197] With such a construction of the Fourteenth Amendment, state inaction permitting patent discrimination, as well as state action, are constitutionally outlawed, necessitating federal intervention to assure equal protection for the black. The Supreme Court in the *Civil Rights Cases* held that state action *openly* or *directly* displayed was prohibited by the Fourteenth Amendment, but a wide hole was left, permitting indirect or camouflaged discrimination that was not state sponsored. Such an interpretation preserves the basic concept of state rights, except that minorities face great difficulty. Professor Commager takes the position that states are a greater threat to freedom than the federal government and state right advocates seek to prevent federal interference to allow the continuance of wrongdoing.[198]

Justice Harlan in his dissenting opinion in the *Civil Rights Cases* suggested that the reach of the Fourteenth Amendment was sufficiently broad to protect the black from private discrimination if the courts would seek diligently to uncover state action. Hotels, railroads, and other industries are regulated by special rules and promoted by government bounty, indicating to Justice Harlan that state and industry are partners so to speak. Separating private and public discrimination is made difficult with such an approach.

While proponents of the state rights concept prevailed in the *Civil Rights Cases,* federal laws had been enacted diminishing state influence. The National Banking Act of 1864 provided for the regulation of national banks to protect the depositor.[199] The Morrill Land-Grant College Act of 1862 gave federal land to states to foster agriculture and engineering.[200] The Contract Labor Act of 1885 helped to recruit labor needed by industry.[201] The Homestead Act of 1862 provided that land would be given free of charge to citizens of the United States.[202] The Morrill Tariff Act of 1861 protected goods manufactured in the United States[203] and the Mining Claims Act of 1866[204] granted mining rights to individuals.

The *Dred Scott*[205] decision to some degree interferes with state rights. Each state was permitted to reject or welcome slavery and the Supreme Court ruled that a black could be pursued into a state banning slavery. If pursuit is permitted into a nonslave state, the state sanctioning slavery imposes its will on others. While this type of rationale can be overstressed, it is nevertheless indicative that state rights cannot be the paramount consideration in many instances.

A damaging aspect of the *Civil Rights Cases* was the failure of the Supreme Court to provide moral leadership for industry and unions. The important Supreme Court decisions are more than an answer to specific questions and contestants—the future action of society is channeled. For example, the Supreme Court decision in 1954 condemning segregation in public schools created a moral tone disproving the claim that segregation can be equal.[206] Not only does segregated schooling lead to inequality in the classroom, but in each distinctive line of endeavor. But the Supreme Court decision in 1896 in *Plessy v. Ferguson*[207] told a white society that segregation was proper and discrimination inevitable and necessary. *Plessy* implies that segregation is desirable and the black less worthy than the white. In the schoolroom, segregation implies that the black is inferior.

An important function of local government is providing quality education. In our society, education is the key to economic opportunity, which in turn determines social status and political power. While the black before 1954 could count on some court help to acquire an education (albeit an inferior education), the Supreme Court stand in the *Civil Rights Cases* negatively affected the black in industry. Unless the economist is correct— that the employer seeks the most efficient employee irrespective of color to

47

maximize profits (the validity of this hypothesis is disputable)—the *Civil Rights Cases* took away from the black the incentive to excel in the classroom.

Few in our society are interested in securing an education without anticipating some economic benefit. If an education cannot lead to tangible benefit, few are motivated to perform well. To the black, *Plessy* and the *Civil Rights Cases* are hypocritical pronouncements—equal education is a constitutional must, yet profit from education is not to be anticipated. Based on *Plessy*, it is possible to assure blacks that the same space, books, and teachers would be provided for black and white. While such equality would require superhuman effort, nevertheless "separate but equal" is possible. But the will to excel in the classroom is more important than bricks and mortar and the Supreme Court in the *Civil Rights Cases* had taken away black incentive to excel by holding that private industry could discriminate. A realistic conclusion is that the absence of economic benefit for the black automatically meant that schooling for black and white would be unequal. The black was dealt a double whammy—not only was education denied in slavery, but the motivation to excel in the classroom was taken away when the Fourteenth Amendment was interpreted to support job discrimination. Even today, the black will not try to excel in the classroom unless industry is able to assure him a fair and equal opportunity.

The *Civil Rights Cases* continued the stamp of black inferiority, a doctrine more forcefully set forth by the Supreme Court in *Dred Scott*,[208] and later implemented in *Plessy*. In *Dred Scott*, the Supreme Court specifically said that the black is inferior, without any rights entitled to protection; the Supreme Court even reasoned that the black was enslaved for his own good. (After *Dred Scott*, the General Land Office ruled that blacks could not qualify for land rights.[209]) If the black is inferior and *Plessy* permits segregated schooling, then inequality in the job marketplace is inevitable. The *Civil Rights Cases* was decided at a time when the black could only look forward to agricultural employment and the industrial employer was told, together with *Dred Scott* and *Plessy*, that the black was inferior.

The black looking at *Dred Scott, Civil Rights Cases, Plessy*, and other decisions could hardly develop respect for our legal, political, and private institutions; the scales of justice were clearly tipped in favor of the white. The *Civil Rights Cases* signifies that in spite of the Civil War and the idealistic ring of the Thirteenth, Fourteenth, and Fifteenth Amendments, the Supreme Court was unwilling to support a theory where equality was more than a pious mouthing. The *Civil Rights Cases* and other decisions stand for the approval of a two-tier society in which the leftovers were reserved for the black.

Another implication of the *Civil Rights Cases* is the Supreme Court call for judicial restraint where discrimination is a factor. Judicial restraint, neutrality if you will, is an indefinable concept, often schizophrenic. When Congress fails to pass legislation to fill a pressing need, critics consider this irresponsible or shabby politics. This is not considered restraint but the abnegation of responsibility. Why the judiciary, and not other branches of government, is obliged to exercise self-restraint is sometimes difficult to explain.[210] That the white was unwilling to grant equality to the black cannot be denied and judicial "neutrality" was best suited to achieve this goal. The Supreme Court knew that the black wallowed in an economic quagmire and had never been a "special favorite of the law."[211] Consequently, judicial restraint must be taken as a cover to prevent change; all too often judicial restraint is the rocking chair approach that protects the status quo.

A by-product of the *Civil Rights Cases* was the signal to industry and unions that discrimination against the black would not be questioned by federal authorities. Du Bois reports that in 1902 not one black was a member of a national union.[212] Irrespective of how damaging its employment policies to blacks, the firm was not to be questioned, handing industry life-and-death power over the economic and political well-being of many people. Industry took good care of its economic and political interests, seeking significant government aid, while government turned its cheek to industry wrongdoing. In several studies made since 1945, the preponderance of evidence points to discrimination being the rule rather than the exception.[213] Although these studies are of recent vintage, it can be assumed that racial discrimination was at least as rampant during the nineteenth and beginning of the twentieth century.

There is a public interest in private employment to assure indigents economic opportunity.[214] But the predominant laissez-faire attitude toward industry until the birth of Keynesian economics and legal doctrine prevented interference in the job market.

The Industrial Revolution signaled economic opportunity for all, and the black had a right to participate. The changing character of industry ended an era of the small and predominantly local entrepreneur and lessened the difficulty of integrating the black into the work force. The changing industrial complex heralded the need for a change in the regulation of industry destined to operate on a nationwide scale. The failure or lack of interest by Congress and the Supreme Court to appreciate fully the changes taking place meant that large-scale industry could not be adequately regulated by the state and laissez faire could no longer be tolerated as a biblical command. The lag between changes taking place and industrial regulation, while injurious to society generally, was particularly damaging to the black. Initial industrial growth in the South did not match growth in the

North, creating a situation in which the southern black was a threat to the white worker.[215] While the Industrial Revolution shoved aside the Jacksonian fear of big business, neither Congress nor the Supreme Court fully appreciated the implications of the dawning era.

To explain developments after the Civil War, it was suggested that the Supreme Court tried to assuage the hard feeling between southern states and the federal government.[216] If true, the black paid dearly for this attempted reconciliation by the judiciary. With tension rising because of economic, social, and political changes, changes difficult to deal with under the best of circumstances, responsibility and leadership were abrogated by the federal government and, specifically, the judiciary.

CHAPTER FIVE ❖ THE PAINFUL SHIFT

Significant change took place after the Civil War, affecting the black and white. While the Industrial Revolution heralded the growth of industry and the centralization of power, agricultural interests continued to swing political power disproportionate to their economic and numerical importance. The manpower needs of industry and technology led to a massive move from a predominantly rural to an urban society. The manpower needs of industry during World War I and II enticed many southern blacks into the city. The bubble of economic hope rested in industry and the more adventuresome black left familiar but less rewarding haunts. Some blacks in the South were better off than blacks in the North, who had to compete with immigrant labor. The manpower needs of industry and the black quest for opportunity drew them together in a manner that would necessitate future government intervention. While the black and industry were slowly drawn together, the prevailing economic, political, and legal attitudes worshipped the successful businessman with scant attention to the black. As public policy shifted to reflect concern with individual welfare, friction was inevitable.

A second event of significance was ushered in by the 1930 depression. Microeconomic theory in fashion prior to the 1930 depression favored freedom for the employer and marketplace without government regulation of competition. While expected to protect and promote, government was to keep out of the way of business. As previously indicated, economic theory went hand-in hand with the prevailing Protestant Ethic and legal theory, which favored a few achievers because society presumably benefited. The basic concept underlying microeconomic theory was that society was well-served by competing businessmen forced to lower prices and develop new products to gain competitive advantage. By lowering product prices and wages, demand would be whetted and more people hired. In this manner, the industrialist became a public benefactor, reducing prices and providing employment.

This microeconomic theory, given the overwhelming prejudice in our society, inevitably prolonged injury to the black. Economic theory strongly influenced political and legal thought, and the worship of laissez faire did nothing to discourage industry and union discrimination. With private dis-

51

133765

crimination rampant and state and federal governments unwilling to intercede, the black was helpless.

Modern Socioeconomic Theory

Classical and neoclassical economists ignored the total level of economic activity, concentrating on the firm. Price and output of the individual firm or in specific markets were the major points of concentration rather than aggregate output. They examined the interaction of supply and demand in particular markets, but not in the economy as a whole. Unfortunately, micro theory, oriented to the individual firm, was used to support national policy and legal doctrine.

The major proposition concerning aggregate economic activity was summed up in Say's Law that "Supply creates its own demand." Supply presumably creates its own demand through the price mechanism. If, at the going price, some goods offered for sale are not purchased, the price will fall and buyers will be induced to buy. If there is unemployment, the wage rate will fall, more people will be hired, and unemployment will disappear. If Say's Law is operative, there is no such thing as unemployment, or at least no such thing as a significant amount of unemployment for any length of time.

The fact that aggregate economic activity was characterized by cyclical and recurring depressions and unemployment did not invalidate Say's Law for most economists. These depressions were treated as infrequent periods of disequilibrium, the tendency of the economy being toward equilibrium; that is, the supply and demand for goods are equal. With unemployment, adjustments would begin and jobs would become available. The natural forces of the market were believed to be the best way of achieving equilibrium. While some depressions were inevitable, government interference was presumed disruptive and harmful; attempts to interfere would make the depression worse or slow down the adjustment process.

According to this reasoning, the public should not be too concerned about occasional periods of high unemployment because they would soon disappear. This may be comforting to the majority of the population who will not be seriously affected by unemployment, but to those who lose their jobs there is little comfort in these words. The people in the latter category are primarily those with low skill or those who are discriminated against in employment opportunities. Therefore, a much higher percentage of blacks than whites are affected by increases in unemployment. Once again, economists ignored the poverty of the black because presumably nothing could be done about it.

After World War I, criticism could be found of traditional economic thought. This skepticism took three forms. In the first place, there was doubt that unemployment needed to be as frequent and severe. Secondly, there were economists who, while agreeing that falling wages and prices would eventually eliminate unemployment, felt that the adjustment process was too slow. Thirdly, some economists doubted that the adjustment process would ever work. They felt that society was doomed to periods of prolonged unemployment unless the government was willing to take a hand in the marketplace.

Evidence supporting each position was found in the Great Depression of the 1930s, which affected every industrialized nation in the world. Governments could not afford to remain neutral and do nothing about poverty and unemployment. In the United States, the New Deal featured many programs intended to alleviate the situation. Unfortunately, many of them did not work, especially the monetary and fiscal programs of the early years of Roosevelt's presidency. They were, in large measure, based upon misconceptions of classical economics. However, in 1936, as the Administration began to pinpoint monetary and fiscal shortcomings, *The General Theory of Employment, Interest and Money*, by John Maynard Keynes, was published, justifying the need for a vigorous role by the federal government to stabilize and improve conditions.[217]

Keynes felt that the hypothesis that unemployment would disappear was inaccurate. He argued further that monetary policy, a policy instrument governments had used to modify business cycles, would not always be able to restore full employment to an economy. Keynes showed why it was sometimes necessary for the federal government to stabilize the economy through fiscal policy, i.e., the combination of its spending and taxing policies.

This theory provided the rationalization for the *tremendous* impact of federal spending during World War II. While Keynes' theory has been modified and corrected since 1936, his principles are essentially unchanged and have been the basis for the direction of federal stabilization policy since World War II.

The basis for the break between Keynes' theory and classical economics can be found in the meaning of the word "unemployment" and in the concept of flexibility of wages. Keynes' reasoning on these issues enabled him to explain how there could be extended periods of unemployment, or even "economic equilibrium" with high unemployment, until the proper fiscal policy was pursued.

In classical economic theory, unemployment led to falling wage rates. This would happen because those seeking work would offer their services for lower and lower wage rates. As wage rates fell, employers would be willing to hire more men, while some people would stop seeking employment because of the lower wage rates. This process continued until there were no more people seeking work. Thus, unemployment was automatically eliminated by the decrease in wages which both increased employment and decreased the number of people seeking work. In this framework, it made no sense to talk about "economic equilibrium" in which there was unemployment. Unemployment is more than not having a job; clearly a four-year-old child is not unemployed, nor is a housewife who does not wish to work. Unemployment means not having a job and wanting to have one. In classical economics, this also meant being willing to work for whatever wage was available as long as it was greater than zero. Therefore, by definition, it was impossible to be unemployed for very long; embodied in the term "unemployed" was the willingness to offer one's services for a lower and lower wage until a job was found.

If one is already on the low end of the wage scale, as most blacks have been, the prescription of lower wages in order to end unemployment is a bitter one. If one was not willing to work for lower wages when out of a job, he was not considered unemployed. He was, instead, a person without a job who was not seeking employment; many blacks have found themselves in this situation. Unwilling to accept the most menial jobs and the lowest wages, they do not have a job, but by the classical definition they are not unemployed. In addition, the black working for less than the white threatened the white community, leading to constant antagonism.

Keynes emphasized that wage rates were not necessarily flexible enough to accommodate all who sought employment. Aside from any normative questions about low wage rates, he said that wage rates did not fall, or did not fall enough, in recessions or depressions to restore full employment. It is possible to argue about the reasons for this (unions, long-term contracts, personal pride) but it is hard to deny that wages are not as flexible as is assumed in classical economics. It is also hard to deny that there was excessively high unemployment during the 1930s which did not disappear.

Keynesian theory holds that aggregate demand must be increased in order to reduce unemployment and, accordingly, increase the level of national income. Aggregate demand is the total amount of goods and services which the members of the economy wish to purchase. One method of raising aggregate demand is for the government to buy more goods and services. The increase in government expenditures immediately raises the level of employment in areas where there is government spending. Additionally, the wages and profits earned from these projects create additional buying power which, in turn, creates more employment, wages, and profits which, in turn, create more buying power, etc. The end result of this "multiplier effect" is that aggregate demand and, therefore, national incomes increase considerably more than the increase in government spending. This, of course, presumes that taxes have not been raised in order to finance the increased governmental expenditures.

Aggregate demand can also be affected by changing the tax rates. A decrease in taxes increases the amount of money consumers have to spend and, therefore, increases the level of aggregate demand. The first round of increased spending due to a tax decrease raises employment, wages, and profits and this initiates the same type of multiplier effect previously mentioned.

The most volatile element in aggregate demand is investment in physical capital, i.e., plant and equipment. Keynesian economics holds that recessions and unemployment occur because people want to save more than they want to invest in new equipment. This means that the public buys less than the economy can supply or that aggregate demand is less than aggregate supply. Government action becomes necessary whenever private investment falls off.

Much government spending, such as that for dams and post office buildings, is simply public investment. Almost all government spending stimulates some private investment due to the additional employment and the workings of the multiplier. The same is true for tax reductions.

An alternative or supplementary policy affects the level of private investment directly. One way is through tax incentives, such as the 7 per cent investment tax credit of recent vintage. Another approach is through the use of monetary policy. The fundamental principle behind monetary policy is that an increase in the money supply lowers the interest rate. This in turn leads to increased investment in new physical capital because of the lower price of borrowed money.

By the 1930s, many economists realized that monetary policy could be used to stabilize the economy. Keynes, however, argued that regulating the money supply and the interest rate would not always increase investment —under certain conditions the interest rate could not be lowered. This is due to the speculative demand for money and Keynes' famous "liquidity trap."[218] According to this theory, there is a certain low, but positive, interest rate at which the yield on securities is so low that people with money will not buy more securities. If additional money is pumped into the system, prospective investors will simply wait. The practical consequence of the "liquidity trap" is that monetary authorities cannot force the interest rate any lower. Therefore, the government cannot bring about additional investment in capital equipment. The merits of the "liquidity trap" theory have been debated at great length. However, whether this particular point of view is accepted or not, most Keynesian economists have doubted the efficacy of monetary policy. In fact, most economists in the past thirty years have placed considerably more emphasis on fiscal policy than monetary policy, although the events of the past several years have raised some doubt about the wisdom of this.

Keynes' theory provided a rationalization for government attempts to affect the level of national income through spending, taxing, and changing the interest rate. In the 1930s and 40s, the emphasis was on spending. During this period, the federal government's role in the economy changed radically.

In 1929, federal spending amounted to $2.6 billion or 2.5 per cent of gross national product (GNP). In 1935, it rose to $6.5 billion or 9.0 per cent of GNP. During World War II, federal expenditure increased even more dramatically, reaching a peak of $95.5 billion or 45.4 per cent of GNP in 1945. It fell to a postwar low of 12.9 per cent of GNP in 1947 and has been above that figure ever since, fluctuating between 17.1 and 21.2 per cent since 1951.[219]

The federal government's involvement in the economy took on additional dimension in the 1930s. New Deal legislation included the NRA (Blue Eagle), Norris-La Guardia Act, Wagner Act, Social Security Act, and Fair Labor Standards Act, which brought public policy to the level of the individual firm. At a state level, possibly because of the limited notion then existing of the interstate commerce clause, workmen's compensation and unemployment compensation laws were passed to put instant oomph into the economy. People unable to work were now given some money to spend. This new brand of economics had to lead to an expanded concept of interstate commerce if the federal government was to wage war effectively on unemployment. In short, government leadership and power were required to direct and influence industry and union decisions.

The federal government had reached into many more sectors of the economy and on a larger scale than previously. Federal impact was so large that its responsibility could no longer be ignored.

The realization of this was manifested in the passage of the Employment Act of 1946. This Act established the Council of Economic Advisors, the Joint Economic Committee of the Congress, and required the President to pursue policies designed to maintain high levels of employment, production, and purchasing power. This is surely a dramatic break with the tradition of classical economics and laissez faire. It also represents a significant change in public policy which affects the welfare of those on the lower end of the income distribution and, thus, a large number of blacks. Unemployment and falling wages to eliminate unemployment are no longer accepted as inevitable. It was the poor man and black man who suffered most when unemployment and falling wages were accepted as inevitable and the poor and the black should benefit most from this change in attitude. However, there were and still are many problems to be solved. This is true concerning most economic problems, but it is especially valid with respect to the black American. Some progress has been made, but the black standard of living is well below that for the average white.

Microeconomic theorists failed to take into account the special circumstances of the black. Since the black held the low-paying job, the employer holding down or cutting wages presumably acted in a prudent manner, paying the market wage, and an obligation to provide for advancement was foreign to the economist. Being without skill, easily displaced, and living in the South where industrial growth was slow, the average black suffered more than the white. The fact that employers—and this included public employers—paid the black less than the white for the same work was conveniently overlooked or shrugged off as a sign of the superior bargaining power of the employer. Economists continued to use the assumption that the employer wants the best man to maximize profits, which supposedly protects the black. That the employer was a member of a society in which discrimination was widespread was ignored. That the employer and others prevented the black from acquiring skill was never mentioned by the theorist. Where part of a group is labeled inferior, the worker must be outstanding before being treated as a superior employee even if the best man theory has some validity. That few can be labeled truly superior went unmentioned.

The black has moved rapidly into the forefront in college and professional sports, an indication to some that ability is the important factor everywhere. However, the comparison of athletics with employment in industry is out of order. The abilities of the star athlete are exposed, to be seen by performer and spectator alike. The black athlete is able to display his value to his teammates—his ability increases earnings for other performers and management. Furthermore, athletic ability can be developed even though discrimination is practiced. In the school, neighborhood club, and on the street, the athlete blessed with natural talent can develop. Performance in the plant, however, is not easily exposed or measured—there are no stars on the production line. And society does not worship the production worker who is destined to leave this earth without fame or fortune. Industry hopes for a normal day's work; in fact co-workers in the plant will not tolerate a star performer. Let any black try to outproduce a white in the plant and the "Black Hand" of industry, the scab label and worse, will be his reward.

Other differences can be pointed to distinguishing the athlete and factory hand. Star athletes are hard to come by whereas the satisfactory employee in the plant is not a rare bird. The spotlight on the athlete, who bows to age and new competitors, is temporary. Thus, the black athlete is not a permanent threat. In the plant, with seniority and other job protection, the black is a worker permanently displacing a white. The theatrical entertainer, academician, and scientist are much like the athlete. These are people with some talent who undergo a period of training considerably longer than the average jobholder in the plant.

A sociologist has reached a conclusion that conflicts, at least to some extent, with the assumption of the economist preaching the best man theory. Professor Blalock holds:

1. The more important and visible the performance of the performer, the lower the degree of employer discrimination.
2. Where performance is easily evaluated, discrimination is reduced.
3. Where high-level performance by the black does not lead to power over the white, discrimination diminishes.
4. There is less discrimination when white co-workers cannot turn to more prestigious jobs (like the professional athlete who finds it difficult to turn to a more prestigious calling).
5. Discrimination abates where the white cannot prevent the black from acquiring the necessary skill.[220]

Some claim that the black is lazy and unable to learn a skill, absolving the white of responsibility for the lack of black progress. Yet, a criticism of the black often heard in the South was that he monopolized the skilled jobs in the construction industry. Slaveowners looked upon the black as inferior while training him, when needed, to perform skilled work. More rationally, the black does not develop skill because he is prevented by the white. Or if morale in the plant might be upset by the presence of a black, the employer claims that he justifiably discriminates to protect his profits.

The shift from laissez faire to Keynesian economics was important to the black because capital investment and full employment became a government responsibility. Where discrimination prevented employment or led to underemployment, government correction was necessary to implement the new policy. The *Civil Rights Cases* decision was made at a time when the employer was the chief beneficiary of government bounty. Government responsibility toward the individual and minorities took a back seat while freedom for industry was the key concern. Following Keynesian philosophy, there is no quicker spender than the black with less income and savings than the white. Money in the hand of the black was sure to be spent, creating more jobs for others. Sociologically, the black was a fast spender, possibly seeking status within and outside his community, a factor currently recognized by the Black Muslims. While the Employment Act of 1946 does not mention color, it assumes particular significance to the black, especially with an upswing in his political power.

A third event promising change beneficial to the black was World War II. World War II was not only a war to prevent a racist empire in Europe, but a humanitarian war to stop man's inhumanity to man because of religion. The position of the United States during World War II was untenable, billing itself as the defender of democracy—democracy and equality were missing in its own back yard. If Uncle Sam could not stay out of the fracas in Europe, the previous hands-off policy followed in its own back yard was no longer politically feasible. Conceding that the prime concern of the United States was stopping German expansion in Europe, the highlighting of Nazi brutality focused attention on the black. When all branches of government ignore, by remaining "neutral," the well-being of black citizens, a parallel with Nazi Germany can be drawn. The "good" German citizen claimed ignorance or an inability to stop the bestiality of the Hitler regime, an approach perfected in the United States toward the black. Educators also completely ignored or swept away the white containment of the black.

Indifference is not neutrality—when the judge acknowledges wrongdoing and turns away from it, he knows that the wrongdoing continues. A natural law or ethical approach leads to an acknowledgment of responsibility for inhumanity and the seeking of a cure, an approach troubling the traditionally trained economist and legal practitioner. Even today, attempts made to correct social ills are "scientifically" criticized—but only infrequently will alternative solutions be proposed other than that the responsibility belongs elsewhere. The Supreme Court of the nineteenth and early twentieth century turned away from wrongdoing and those later sitting on the Bench felt that atonement was in order. In many ways, economic and legal thinking was rigidified. As stated by a talented psychiatrist:

> What I call middle-class society is any society that becomes rigidified in predetermined forms, forbidding all evolution. . . . I call middle-class a closed society in which life has no taste. . . . And I think that a man who takes a stand against this death is in a sense a revolutionary.[221]

Strategically, the time was ripe to force fair employment by putting the spotlight on inequity in the United States. For the first time, large numbers of black leaders had not been killed off by white racists. Led by Mr. Randolph of the Sleeping Car Porters Union, a march of 50,000 blacks was threatened in 1942 on Washington, D.C.[222] Warring to protect democracy, Uncle Sam could ill afford worldwide adverse publicity, a factor known to black strategists. Furthermore, the shortage of labor during wartime placed the black in a good position to insist on fair employment. President Roosevelt was forced to settle the threatened conflict quickly and satisfactorily.

Welders, electrical workers, machinists, sheet metal workers, etc., were needed during World War II, and few blacks were available with these skills.[223] The shortage of skilled and general labor opened jobs to the black, but few could move into the more lucrative occupations. Trade schools in the South did not train the black for industry—he was fitted for domestic and other trades requiring a minimum of skill. Southern trade schools were poorly equipped. In the North, the better vocational schools were in white neighborhoods, which automatically excluded the black. Neither employers nor unions trained blacks.

Craft unions in the North and South influenced vocational training. These unions operated in a discriminatory manner, and black training was bound to reflect this prejudice. The federal (and state) government was not an innocent bystander, providing almost one-half of the funds allocated to vocational education, knowing that discrimination was flagrant.

A fourth factor forced the federal government to reach into the market-place. In 1890, 90.3 per cent of all blacks, 7½ million, lived in the South, 60 per cent attached to agriculture and 30 per cent holding service jobs.[224] By 1930, 60 per cent of the blacks lived in the city, and the migration continued during World War II. The black by 1960 was concentrated in a dozen cities in which the crime and unemployment rates were high; the white fled to the suburb, increasing the political power of the black; and black leadership became more effective because of geographic concentration. The younger and better-educated black, unwilling to accept slow and gradual improvement and claiming entitlement to opportunity, knew that the white was unwilling to share his economic bounty.[225] Equally important to the black community was a showing that some control could be exercised over its destiny and that change could be forced. Concentrated in a few small areas, black dissatisfaction and white fear of disturbance was accentuated. Government was forced to play a hand; traditional stands of laissez faire and neutrality were not feasible, especially since commitment to the black was historically limited. Killings, mayhem, destruction of property and deterioration of the city necessitated greater government intervention.

The numerically and economically superior white community has to show more willingness to correct past injustice and more understanding of black methods. Overnight rectification of past injustice is unfortunately impossible under the best of circumstances—many in the black community understand this; what may be important is a show of good faith by the white, a willingness to share economic bounty and political power. To show good faith, the white community must be willing to make concessions and permit reverse discrimination. But the black is unconvinced that the white will accept him as an economic and political equal—this evaluation is probably accurate—while the white community is unable to adjust to the increased disruption.

Society adjusts to wide-reaching technological change and the endless state of war but seems unable to adjust to the black revolution. Pointing to methods used by blacks to instigate change rather than to the underlying causes, white backlash follows. Our society, it appears, is much more tolerant of "white collar crime" than physical crime. From a sociological, rather than a legal, perspective, prejudice resulting in discrimination is tantamount to a criminal act.

The Political Attack

After the assassination of President Lincoln, Congress was swept away by the upswell of emotion in the North and responded legislatively: the Civil Rights Act of 1866,[226] the Enforcement Act of 1870,[227] the Klu Klux Klan Act of 1871,[228] and the Civil Rights Act of 1875.[229] (Somewhat similar sympathy was shown after the assassination of Dr. King.) But the ardor of society soon cooled, and the impact of these laws was nullified by Supreme Court decisions.[230] Not until World War II, or thereabouts, did the federal government press to benefit the black. For more than fifty years, the black was told to shift for himself in a society unwilling to accept him.

As previously indicated, a new era dawned during the 1930 depression when the federal government adopted Keynesian economics and the WPA was created to provide jobs for black and white. The first clear political signal of change, in 1939, favorable to the black, was the little heralded Civil Rights Section within the Department of Justice. The makeup of Congress prevented legislative action in circumstances begging for legislative change, and the Executive Branch of government was forced to take the initiative. The Supreme Court as yet had given little notice that it would champion civil rights; in fact, an examination of past decisions was enough to label it a negative force.

Some of the legislation passed after the Civil War was not guillotined by the Supreme Court and the Civil Rights Section dusted it off for use.[231] The initial thrust of the Civil Rights Section was aimed at voting[232] and police brutality. Due to prior Supreme Court decisions and operating with a small staff and budget, the reach of the Civil Rights Section was limited to employment, housing, and schooling. On the whole, the Civil Rights Section accomplished little before World War II. The Civil Rights Section began to swing its weight in civil rights practically unnoticed after World War II through the *amicus curiae* brief.

The *amicus curiae* brief is something of an anomaly in light of the political concept of separation of power between executive, legislative, and judicial branches of government. The executive branch of government participates in the judicial process by spelling out its position, via the *amicus curiae* brief, and executive and judicial "cooperation" can make up for a Congress unconcerned with black welfare. Although considerable authority is delegated to the Attorney General, it must be presumed that jumping into

61

the civil rights arena was authorized by the President. While criticized for not helping the black during World War II until forced to and for allowing citizens of Japanese ancestry to be moved from the West Coast, President Roosevelt did approve of the Civil Rights Section.

The Supreme Court did not formulate rules regulating the *amicus curiae* brief until 1937.[233] As the federal regulation of commerce expanded, the use of *amicus curiae* expanded, closely linked to the civil rights movement. *Amicus curiae* shifted from a device to lend a friendly hand to the judiciary to a means of benefiting minorities by permitting considerable "judicial lobbying."[234] The *amicus curiae* brief and oral pleading are used more frequently to protect civil rights than in other kinds of litigation. The political overtones of *amicus curiae* cannot be overstressed since many Supreme Court decisions lead to wide-reaching change. Private persons interested in the outcome of a case and those inadequately protected can intervene in a federal court, while the Department of Justice has carte blanche authority to step into any case via the *amicus curiae* route and plead orally.[235]

The Executive Branch of government can also encourage legislative change. For example, President Eisenhower, recovering from a heart attack in 1955, was not interested in tough civil rights legislation, but Attorney General Brownell, cognizant of the big city vote, saw the need for pressing for a stronger hand. This led to the Civil Rights Act of 1957.[236] In the courtroom, and particularly before the Supreme Court, the role played by the Department of Justice in the Civil Rights arena should not be underestimated. For example, the Civil Rights Section has already participated as an *amicus* in many cases involving Title VII of the Civil Rights Act.[237] Under Title VII, the Equal Employment Opportunity Commission (EEOC) is without enforcement power and the Civil Rights Section must assume greater responsibility to assure fair employment where there is a "pattern" of discrimination.[238]

Not only is the ruling power of the executive branch of government expanded during wartime, but, in addition, the federal government buys large quantities of goods from industry when, officially, we are not at war. When world unrest and military preparedness continue, the President can hit at unfair employment by letting contracts to industry, insisting upon fair employment. Starting with President Roosevelt during World War II, and continuing to the present, every president has decreed that all government contracts let to industry contain a clause calling for fair employment.[239]

Executive Order 11246, issued in 1965, authorizes the Secretary of Labor to enforce government contracts calling for fair employment. He can blacklist employers who continue to discriminate, sue for violation of contract, etc.

In 1968, the Office of Federal Contracts Compliance (OFCC) in the Department of Labor provided guidelines for industry to follow on government contracts in excess of $10,000.[240] In addition, contractors employing more than fifty were required to maintain records showing efforts made to hire blacks.[241] The OFCC has referred at least two possible violations to the Department of Justice and suits have been brought.[242]

The Federal Aviation Agency has required all airports constructed with federal money to be built by a fair employer since 1964.[243] In 1966, the Treasury Department ordered all banks safeguarding government funds or acting as a financial agent not to discriminate in employment or deposits would be removed.[244] This order, applying to 12,000 banks with federal deposits in excess of $4 billion,[245] came after a study made in 1966 disclosed that less than one per cent of the white-collar help in banks was black. Federal funds have been withdrawn from banks refusing to cooperate.[246]

The Federal Communications Commission announced that licenses will be denied to applicants seeking to operate radio and television stations who are uninterested in fair employment.[247] The Commission is obligated to investigate charges of discrimination before issuing a license, and Title VII of the Civil Rights Act applies to all station operators hiring more than 25 employees. Title VII covers 80 to 90 per cent of the television stations and 10 per cent of the radio stations. Black talent, the well-known performer, is seen frequently on television, but few blacks have been seen in the lesser roles and advertisements until recently. Few blacks with technical skill have been hired to work backstage in the radio and television stations. The failure to hire the black in an expanding industry like television is nothing new —merely another sample of white dominance in jobs holding financial promise.

Television ridicule and exposure can help to pave the way for equality, showing the black as a person with all the strengths and weaknesses of the white. Furthermore, poking fun at prejudice and zeroing in on discrimination help to prevent complacency. But television exposure of prejudice without fair employment by the networks, advertising agencies, and advertisers only points to white hypocrisy.

Federal authorities supply much of the operating budget of state operated employment offices.[248] Uncle Sam insists that the state offices of the United States Employment Services (USES) cater to fair employers only. Nevertheless, state agencies continue to serve unfair employers at public expense. Because there is a possible violation of the Fifth and Fourteenth Amendments and Title VII, private citizens or civil rights organizations should challenge unfair placements by the USES.

The state employment agencies continue to serve unfair employers for the following reasons:

1. White employees and administrative officials of the USES are not interested in fair employment.[249]
2. Employees of the USES are more interested in maintaining good relations with employers than in black welfare.
3. The USES is slow to investigate a charge of discrimination and cannot punish meaningfully the unfair employer.
4. The efficiency rating of a USES employee depends somewhat on the number of employees successfully placed. The USES placement officer, to protect his efficiency rating, will not make a referral to a known unfair employer.
5. An employer can claim that a black is inefficient, which is not checked by the USES.
6. To spare the feeling of a black, USES employees will not make a referral to an unfair employer.
7. Employees of the USES are sensitive to local conditions.

Increased cooperation between the EEOC or state commissions and the USES could help to reduce discrimination. By investigating, without fanfare, placements of the USES, the EEOC or state commission could pinpoint the source of discrimination.[250] Employers guilty of discrimination should be publicized and/or blacklisted, denying them the use of government facilities. In addition, state or federal charges could be preferred. Investigators of the EEOC or state commissions could concentrate on the largest employers using the USES, maximizing benefit to the black. Investigators should check the number of blacks referred to the employer by the USES, the number of blacks seeking referral at the USES, the number and type of jobs held by blacks, etc. At the very least, such investigations would offer evidence of the success of the USES in finding jobs for blacks and the type of referrals made.

Thirty to 40 per cent of all jobs are filled by employees referring their friends.[251] If most employees are white and blacks are found in the least desirable jobs, the new jobholders are going to be white unless the firm makes an effort to recruit blacks. Where this type of employment pattern appears, the USES, state and federal commissions, and government agencies letting contracts to industry should urge the firm to change its recruiting techniques.

The investigation suggested of USES placements should also be undertaken of the union operating a hiring hall. National leaders of unions, some more willingly and sincere than others, are interested in minimizing discrimination in the House of Labor; some effort has already been made by the AFL-CIO to curb discrimination. In spite of the dedication of some national leaders, locals continue to discriminate. If discrimination at the local level is to be minimized, state and federal officials must show greater interest in the internal operation of unions. The substantial support of Mr. Wallace during the 1968 presidential election by union members indicates a need for protecting the black at the local level.[252] There are differences between the fair employment policy expressed by national leaders and feeling at the local level. While the evidence available is insufficient to condemn all locals, enough is available to initiate precautionary measures.

Where unions operate hiring halls, information is sorely needed to determine the steps that should be taken to assure fair placement. In 1961, the Supreme Court decided that the hiring hall operated in a nondiscriminatory manner, referring union and nonunion men, does not violate section 8 (a) (3) of the Taft-Hartley Act.[253] While the Supreme Court only considered discrimination against nonunion men and transferees from other locals, the hiring hall is used to discriminate against blacks. Too few charges are brought under the Taft-Hartley Act or state or federal fair employment legislation when the ease with which the hiring hall can lead to abuse is considered. Blacks spending a lifetime facing discrimination are unlikely to turn to the union-operated hiring hall to find a job. If, for example, blacks face discrimination in the construction trades unions, they will not enter the union headquarters from which the hiring hall is operated. And many construction trade unions operate a hiring hall.

Whether white or black, nonunion jobseekers are unlikely to enter the lion's den—it is inconceivable to them that the union would be willing to act as a placement agency for them. Furthermore, the nonunion white able to join the union would be losing "face" since he would be conceding that the union performs a valuable service that he should support. But many unions have been closed to blacks and the slow and grudging manner in which membership is made available doesn't create confidence that he will be fairly treated. In fact, the nonjoiner unwilling to contribute support is viewed as an economic leech by union members. For a nonunion man to walk into headquarters to seek employment is bound to be a distasteful experience. Man seeks to avoid pain, and the outsider will be reluctant to walk into union headquarters.

While the Supreme Court correctly gleaned the intent of Congress not to outlaw the hiring hall, for all practical purposes the closed shop is legal where the union is used as the exclusive job referral agent. The EEOC or state commission with investigatory power could perform a valuable service by investigating the hiring hall to determine the number of nonunion men who apply for a job, how many of the applicants are black, the number of blacks referred to jobs, attitude of employer to whom the black is referred, etc. In fact, the evidence uncovered could lead to a suit by the Attorney General under Title VII, claiming a "pattern" of discrimination. The NLRB can entertain an unfair labor practice charge where the hiring hall is used illegally, but it does not have the investigative power of the EEOC. Furthermore, the NLRB decision may not end illegal referrals through the hiring hall. Unless the NLRB outlaws the hiring hall, discrimination can continue in the future. It is possible that the "pattern" of discrimination relief permitted by Title VII is a better remedy than NLRB adjudication since the Attorney General could continue to keep a watchful eye on the union and the court could retain jurisdiction over the defendant. If employers need the hiring hall to assure an adequate supply of skilled labor—one reason assigned by Congress for not outlawing the hiring hall—cancelling by court order the use of the hiring hall forces the employer to take a more active interest in the future to assure its fair use.

Because the hiring hall is arranged by a collective bargaining contract, it may be possible for a black to bring a suit directly in court for breach of contract without going through the EEOC.

While data are not available to show the extent to which the black turns to the union-operated hiring hall, it is our contention that it is not frequent. If our guess is correct, this means that evidence will not be available to show that hiring halls are operated illegally. To break down this threat to fair employment will require interested organizations to push blacks to the hiring hall.

State Action—Oih Veh

The dedication with which the Supreme Court has entered the civil rights foray since World War II is some indication of a willingness to modify the *Civil Rights Cases.* Slowly, but clearly, the Supreme Court has moved in the direction of boxing in the stand taken in the *Civil Rights Cases* without express reversal. In 1945, the Supreme Court, by refusing to grant *certiorari,* upheld a decision that a private institution getting the bulk of its financial support from a state violates the Fourteenth Amendment when blacks are forbidden to use the facilities.[254] In 1946, the Supreme Court found state action when a private corporation dominated the economic and political life of the community.[255]

A landmark decision was *Shelley v. Kraemer*[256] in which the Supreme Court considered the constitutionality of an agreement prohibiting the sale of homes to blacks. Courts had accepted the validity of a racially restrictive covenant,[257] a form of private discrimination, when in 1948 the Supreme Court agreed to take a look. It is interesting to note that the Civil Rights Section, via the *amicus* technique, threw its weight on the side of the black.

Although the Fourteenth Amendment forbids state discrimination only, this limitation can be skirted if the concept of state action is broadly conceived. Such an approach may be more desirable politically than a complete reversal of the *Civil Rights Cases,* appeasing somewhat the worship-

66

pers of freedom in the market place. Furthermore, the jurist clinging to tradition may be satisfied since the *Civil Rights Cases* is not reversed and the Supreme Court is less vulnerable to charges of usurping legislative authority. Nevertheless, such a course of action is painful to plot and the course taken is uncertain even if necessary. Had the Supreme Court reversed the decision in the *Civil Rights Cases*, the judicial line to follow would have been clearer. But if the unwillingness of Congress to initiate change is recognized and there is acceptance of the view that current tempo necessitated shift, the Supreme Court was obligated to take a look at the direction taken by the executive branch of government. Critics of the Supreme Court position in *Shelley* ignore the direction already taken by the executive agencies which did not wait for congressional endorsement. With all due respect to the basic philosophy calling for a separation of the functions of government, action may be essential by one governmental branch when another refuses to move if the need is *clear*. As a point of speculation, would Congress have passed the Civil Rights Act of 1964 (and other legislation) if the executive and judicial branches of government had not already pointed to the need to hit at discrimination? Was Congress shamed into taking a belated stand? Fortunately, the executive and judicial branches of government had a love-in in *Shelley*, easing the pain certain to be caused by pulling away from precedent established in the *Civil Rights Cases*. The willingness of the executive branch of government to enter the cesspool called civil rights must have helped to pave the way for Supreme Court reconsideration.

In *Shelley*, the Supreme Court followed tradition by deciding that the restrictive covenant negotiated by private persons was constitutionally proper even if intended to maintain an all-white turf. The Fourteenth Amendment was violated when the court was asked to enforce the discriminatory agreement; at this point the state participates in the discrimination, necessitating the stopping of "Rosemary's Baby." The Supreme Court in *Shelley* dusted off the dissenting opinion of Justice Harlan in the *Civil Rights Cases* to deal realistically with the turbulence of the twentieth century. When *Shelley* reached the Supreme Court, most blacks lived in big city ghettos, often in the North. The population explosion in the ghetto, by birth and migration, and black militancy required a breakout. Many blacks returning from military service were unwilling to tolerate second-class citizenship, the clear meaning of the *Civil Rights Cases, Plessy,* and others. The black had been localized by racially restrictive covenants and other tactics needing change: slum landlords were gouging the black who had no alternative. The Fourteenth Amendment forbad statutes calling for segregation, but based on the ruling in the *Civil Rights Cases*, private agreements calling for segregation were constitutional. The ghettos were, when *Shelley*

67

arose, already teeming, pointing to the violence to come during the 1960s.

White residents in the big city found many differences in the black to justify geographical segregation, often pointing to the absence of middle-class values. The immigrant from Europe came with middle-class values while black exposure to them was minimal, and he often found them unacceptable. The black out of slavery shared one middle-class value, a desire to own land. When this aspiration was denied, the black fleeing to the urban center and succeeding generations were localized and confined. Subcultural patterns developed in slavery and the ghetto conflicted with white middle-class values. Even if the black came with middle-class values, he would be unacceptable to the white.

Shelley raises the old legal "footsy" question of what is law. What law is (and is not) is a subject debated extensively in the law school and the adjoining pub, but the answer supplied by Justice Holmes, that the law is what the judge says it is, has the most truthful and consistent ring. When the Supreme Court blessed the restrictive covenant as valid, the law was fixed. That an attempt to enforce a valid agreement is constitutionally forbidden is difficult to explain to a layman (and professional). To most, an agreement labeled legal means that it will be enforced by court order if necessary. That this kind of legal shadow boxing is essential to bring about change is difficult to explain to the uninitiated.

Had the Supreme Court so willed it, state involvement could have been detected before the plaintiffs sought an injunction to enforce the restrictive agreement. A covenant running with the land is not binding upon the purchaser unless there is actual or constructive notice of the agreement. So that notice is given to the "world," the restrictive covenant is recorded with the County Clerk where the land is located. Was there state action prohibited by the Fourteenth Amendment when the County Clerk recorded the restrictive covenant? Did the state discriminate when the recorded agreement was permitted to have the widest possible impact? These questions were important in *Shelley* because the black buyer of the property was not aware of the restrictive covenant. The Supreme Court would have clipped even more the reach of the *Civil Rights Cases* if the recording of the restrictive covenant were labeled a violation of the Fourteenth Amendment. If the Supreme Court wished to contain the *Civil Rights Cases* as much as possible, the recording of the covenant was the logical cut-off point. By permitting the recording of the agreement, the County Clerk helps the discriminator. By relying on the concept of constructive notice, the judiciary supports the discriminator. *Shelley*, as it stands, bars some, but not all, state action. Perhaps for this reason some state aid is forbidden and other state aid is permissible. Had the Supreme Court found a constitutional violation when the restrictive agreement was recorded, it can be reasoned that even minimal state aid would be forbidden.

Suppose a realtor develops a large area or suburb and blacks cannot buy a home.[258] There is continual interaction between the developer and city considering the building of sidewalks, police and fire protection, sewers, buildings code, etc., when a new section is under way. Is such interaction sufficient to constitute a violation of the Fourteenth Amendment? Based on *Shelley*, some forms of discrimination are permissible.[259]

In *Rice v. Sioux City Memorial Park*,[260] the Fourteenth Amendment was not violated when the supervisor of a private burial association stopped the interment of a Winnebago Indian. Because there was no participation by the state in the discrimination, the Fourteenth Amendment was inapplicable. Presume that the Indian was buried over the protest of the park director. Could the association get a court order to exhume the body without violating the Fourteenth Amendment? Suppost fighting broke out when the groundkeeper refused to permit burial. Should the Fourteenth Amendment forbid the use of police to remove the mourners and the body?

In a case arising in Michigan, a plaintiff holding burial rights sued a park interfering with the burial of a black. As a defense, the park referred to a restrictive covenant in the burial contract. The court held for the plaintiff, that bowing to the restrictive covenant would constitute state action.[261]

The importance of *Shelley* to the civil rights movement should not be minimized. *Shelley* drew the Supreme Court smack into the "political thicket," deciding what is and what is not state involvement, forcing the judiciary to sit down on the white discriminator. *Shelley* tells the lower courts to assume greater responsibility to end discrimination, that the "judicial restraint" practiced in a bygone era is no longer tolerable. Such an active, in place of the traditionally passive, role called for in *Shelley* inevitably subjects the Supreme Court to increased pressures and criticism. The political implications of *Shelley* are enormous, such as the meaning of state rights; a willingness to find state involvement adds to the federal ability to move in on local discrimination.

The spillover of *Shelley* continues, making itself felt in the electoral system and private employment. In *Terry v. Adams*,[262] a controversy arising under the Fifteenth Amendment, the discriminatory selection of white candidates by the Democratic Party to run for public office wrongfully denied blacks the right to participate in the elective process. In many southern states, receiving the Democratic Party nomination is tantamount to election, so that the Fifteenth Amendment outlaws discriminatory selection made by a private organization (it can be argued that a major political party is a quasipublic or public organization). The Supreme Court in *Shelley* widened the concept of state action, later reflected in *Terry* under the Fifteenth Amendment.

The implications of *Terry* are far reaching, particularly since political and economic success go hand-in-hand. The bulk of the black population resides in a dozen urban centers, leaning toward the Democratic Party in the North.[263] Many blacks, too many, remain poor and uneducated, but there are some who are neither poor nor uneducated. The buying power of blacks annually exceeds 500 million dollars in Houston, 300 million in Atlanta, and 250 million in New Orleans.[264] Political leaders in the northern city appreciate the significance of the black vote, and as more black voters are registered in the South, white political leaders must accommodate the black voter. It is possible that the political implications of the black migration to the urban center have not been fully realized. In many ways, the relationship between state and federal government is an anachronism if technological change, monetary problems of the state and city, large industry and unions, and global involvement of the United States are considered. A search for a more efficient system of government could lead to a conclusion that the state is obsolete, and a more fruitful relationship is possible between a city-state (the sprawling metropolitan area) and the federal government. Since the 1930 depression, the power of the federal government has been growing—and most of this is inevitable and necessary in spite of criticism—rendering state government obsolete, a useless and interfering appendage. *Shelley* and other state action cases point to the obsolescence of state government—the need for federal authority to protect citizens when the state (and/or city) is unwilling to do it.

The philosophy enunciated in *Shelley* can result in the application of the Fourteenth Amendment to unions nurtured and protected by state and federal legislation.[265] For the most part, however, the courts have been unwilling to extend the Fourteenth Amendment to unions practicing discrimination.[266]

An important facet of *Shelley* was the signal, loud and clear, for the lower courts to stretch the meaning of state action and display greater ingenuity in using the Fourteenth Amendment.[267] While the course of action followed has been painful and confusing, the courts have accepted the challenge and the meaning of state action has been expanded since the decision in the *Civil Rights Cases*.[268] Some court decisions have emphasized the extent of state aid; if the aid is not considered substantial, the Fourteenth Amendment is inapplicable. The Fourteenth Amendment does not call for substantial state action, only that there be state action. Admittedly, government today reaches into many private pockets and it is plausible to argue that not all government involvement can be labeled a violation of the Fourteenth Amendment. Nevertheless, undue concern with the extent of state

70

involvement seems pointless in some of the cases. If the whole show is under government direction, courts find a violation of the Fourteenth Amendment without a test of substantiality. But where a private organization is the discriminator, it becomes important, as the courts see it, to check the extent of state responsibility. Evidently, the Supreme Court in *Shelley* found the state involvement substantial.

State aid to private discriminators takes the form of financial assistance, use of state facilities, letting of government contracts, etc. The courts, where financial support is extended to industry, look to the dollars; if not substantial, the Fourteenth Amendment is not violated even though the discriminator receives direct state support. But where unions are involved, organizations attaining political and economic strength because of federal sponsorship, courts are reluctant to invoke the Fifth Amendment. It is possible, however, that this reluctance to find state action where there is union discrimination is in a transitional phase.

Clearly, where the discriminator does not seek state aid, the Fourteenth Amendment cannot be utilized to halt discriminatory practices.[269]

The Supreme Court further boosted the concept of state action in *Burton v. Wilmington Parking Authority*[270] where state inaction was equated with state action on state property. The Supreme Court approach in *Terry v. Adams* was similar. Permitting the Democratic Party to discriminate against blacks when selecting candidates for public office ultimately leads to the state. The discrimination by the Democratic Party did not take place on state property; but, realistically, separating the appointive and elective process on the basis of private and government property is impractical.

In *Burton,* Wilmington officialdom built a multistory parking lot in the city center, with stores available for lease on the ground floor. A store was let to a restaurateur without expressly providing that patrons were to be served without discrimination. The Supreme Court ruled that the failure of the city to negotiate a lease calling for access to the restaurant on a nondiscriminatory basis violated the Fourteenth Amendment. In a nutshell, the failure of the state to protect the black on government property constituted state discrimination.

The approach taken by the Supreme Court in *Wilmington* deviates from past practice. Since the Fourteenth Amendment forbids state action only, without mention of inaction, the reach of the Fourteenth Amendment is stretched a wee bit. In *Shelley,* the recording of a racially restrictive covenant on state property was not called improper. There was in fact more state involvement in *Shelley,* when the covenant was recorded, than in *Wilmington,* where city officials failed to extract a promise from the lessee that all patrons would be served. By trumpeting the need for supervision on public property, the Supreme Court told state officialdom to get off their backside

71

and protect the black. *Wilmington* is a signal that political restraint, whether it be executive, legislative, or judicial, is a cover-up for discrimination and no longer tolerable. It is judicial philosophy calling for state-sponsored attack against discrimination on state property, and that doing nothing is the equivalent of promoting discrimination. As pointed to before, judicial restraint is not neutrality. Such a judicial philosophy would have helped to stop black lynching in the South.

Unanswered in *Wilmington* is whether the Fourteenth Amendment applies when a pronounced pattern of discrimination continues on privately owned property without state effort to end it. In *Wilmington*, the restaurant facility was under the exclusive control of the lessee, a short step from hitting at discrimination on private property. The Fourteenth Amendment is only stretched a wee bit more if state intervention is required to end a pattern of discrimination on privately owned property.

The Supreme Court in *Wilmington* noted that the restaurant was linked closely with the operation of the parking lot. Had the Supreme Court stopped after maintaining that state inaction is the equivalent of state action on government property, less uncertainty would prevail today. Unfortunately, the Supreme Court emphasized that the restaurant and parking lot formed an integral unit. Whether state inaction is tantamount to state action only when private business on public property is an integral part is unanswered. Suppose the state acquires two blocks of property, a parking lot on one block and stores on the second block. If the stores were not built by the state as a connecting link with the parking lot, would the Fourteenth Amendment be violated if a restaurateur refused to serve blacks?

To some degree, *Wilmington* and *Shelley* conflict. In *Shelley*, the restrictive covenant was recorded and the black buyer of the real estate was unaware of the agreement. On government property, in the County Recorder's office, effect was given to the covenant without condemnation by the Supreme Court. In *Wilmington*, a lack of effort to prevent discrimination is state action on government property. The recording of the restrictive covenant and the finding of constructive notice of the agreement is state action (or is it inaction?).

The NLRB, National Mediation Board, and the National Railway Adjustment Board—to name but a few—have tolerated racial discrimination, permitting employers and unions to use government facilities. Employers and unions have petitioned government agencies to hold representation elections, entertain unfair labor practice charges, and appearances have been made on government property. There is merit to the position that the Fifth Amendment, based on *Wilmington*, would be violated if discriminators use federal facilities for personal benefit. Admittedly, the lessee in *Wilmington* was rightfully ensconced on government property during the life of the lease while temporary licensees coming upon government property fit into a different legal pigeonhole. Yet is this difference enough to distinguish *Wilmington* from those organizations using the National Mediation Board or other agency? *Shelley* requires open or direct participation in the discriminatory act while *Wilmington* holds that private discrimination by those using government property cannot be tolerated. Based on *Wilmington,* recording restrictive covenants, entertaining unfair labor practices and certification and decertification proceedings, which take place on government property, could be outlawed under the Fourteenth Amendment.

Squelching another attempt to hem in the black, the Supreme Court, in *Reitman v. Mulkey*,[271] considered the California Proposition 14, permitting homeowners to sell to anyone they wanted to by repealing the state fair housing law and prohibiting the passage of a future state law (except under specially enumerated circumstances) limiting the seller's right to select the buyer.

The Supreme Court ruled that Proposition 14 violated the Fourteenth Amendment, an absence of state neutrality, because it was aimed at the black and there was a denial of equal protection of the law. Not only did Proposition 14 repeal the fair housing law, but enacting one in the future was made difficult. In this manner, the state threw its weight behind white citizens anxious to keep the black in the ghetto in violation of the Fourteenth Amendment. The legislative scheme was intended to localize the black and to neutralize the executive, legislative, and judicial branches of government. Where discrimination in housing is widespread, state neutrality is a myth if the passage of fair housing legislation is stifled. It is interesting to note that the Solicitor General participated in the decision with an *amicus curiae* brief.

As previously pointed to, the Supreme Court in *Jones v. Alfred H. Mayer Co.* seemed to reverse its ruling in the *Civil Rights Cases* by holding that the Thirteenth Amendment could serve as the constitutional crutch for federal legislation, protecting the black seeking to purchase or lease real property. Because of their decision, there is the possibility that Section 1 of the Civil Rights Act of 1866 protects the employment rights of the black. Section 1 gives blacks the same right to enter into a contract as whites and employment can be viewed as a contractual relationship.

For the purpose of the Fourteenth Amendment, the Supreme Court in *Jones* did not reverse or consider its decision in the *Civil Rights Cases.* Since the 1866 legislation was supported by the Thirteenth Amendment, the Supreme Court did not find it necessary to discuss the Fourteenth Amendment. But *Jones* raises a strong possibility that, if necessary, the Supreme Court is ready to expressly reverse its stand in the *Civil Rights Cases.*

The Supreme Court since *Shelley* has consistently attempted to minimize the impact of the *Civil Rights Cases,* although *certiorari* has been denied where the state aid was considered insignificant. The acceptance or rejection of the Supreme Court decisions depends upon legal philosophy, acceptance of the black, etc. This shifting away from the *Civil Rights Cases* since World War II has been consistent and can be accepted as a no-nonsense approach to the elimination of discrimination. To justify the post-World War II approach of the Supreme Court, it can be reasoned that the meaning of state action is fluid rather than rigid; the dividing line between state and private action is shadowy and not definable; the *Civil Rights Cases* inadequately explored the meaning of state action; and state and private action are inevitably intertwined. Cliffhangers are inevitable because the Supreme Court is striking at racial hostility in the public and private sectors, using the prohibition against public discrimination to justify its attack.

Shelley has to be evaluated in terms of modern-day conditions, that private industry is not as private as it used to be. While *Shelley* dealt with the small owner, its impact upon big business should not be lost. If the character of industry has changed since the *Civil Rights Cases,* and it undeniably has, then the judicial interpreter must view the business transaction accordingly. Present-day industry is characterized by the concentration of firms in few hands—witness the torrid increase in horizontal, vertical, and conglomerate mergers taking place since World War II in spite of the efforts of Congress, the Department of Justice, and the Supreme Court. These large firms are active in the political and military arena, holding large government contracts affecting the lives of thousands of employees and the future of the areas in which the firms are housed. As the firm grows larger, wrongdoing, and not just the criminal or contractual type, is less tolerable as damage to society is magnified. Industry reluctantly tackles moral problems and fears taking an open stand on the "unpopular" issue. The large firm was warned in *Shelley* that its activities have to be more closely scrutinized. If it is important to stop discrimination in housing, it is at least equally important to stop unfair employment. In fact, discriminatory employment leads to discriminatory housing.

Technological change invites largeness, but the lack of government direction and laissez-faire philosophy contributed to the concentration of industrial growth. Antitrust legislation has not been effective, partially due to an absence of effective prosecution, court doctrine, and economic theory. In fact, based upon legislative appropriation early in the "ball game," it is doubtful whether Congress seriously considered squelching the growth of the firm. Not only did the federal government fail to provide the wherewithal necessary to prevent concentration, but government spending since the 1930 depression contributed substantially to the present economic concentration. Industries benefiting extensively by government policy are obligated to forcefully follow the moral line. In the military-industrial complex so influential today, separating government and industrial responsibility is not a simple task. When industry is unwilling to take the initiative, government must move in, a consequence of the expanded concept of interstate commerce, economic policy, and reevaluation of past practices. The moral obligation of large industry is no less than that of a government agency. In this sense, the need for a finding of state action under the Fifth or Fourteenth Amendments is obsolete.

Shelley, Wilmington, and other cases structuring the meaning of state action also point to changing conditions in our society, calling for a rethinking of the meaning of separation of power between executive, legislative, and judicial branches of government. Just as political separation between state and federal power is used intentionally to engage in discrimination, executive, legislative, and judicial separation is similarly used. Government discrimination took place in *Shelley* when the restrictive covenant was recorded, an executive function; but, according to the Supreme Court, the state action prohibited by the Fourteenth Amendment was to be laid at the door of the judicial branch of government if the covenant was enforced. The Supreme Court in *Wilmington* cited the misuse of government property controlled by the executive branch of government for failing to assure full use by the black. If a legislative body authorizes the erection of a parking ramp, is the Fourteenth Amendment violated when it fails to provide equal use of all facilities? In a nutshell, each branch of government has been willing to wait for other branches to assume responsibility. The abdication of responsibility is part and parcel of the system of government calling for checks and balances even though the great consensus of opinion endorses the basic system.

The constitutional niceties revolving about our system of checks and balances are ignored when expedient. Congress did not declare war in Vietnam, but, nevertheless, a peace treaty is negotiated while troops fight on. The Supreme Court was able to expand the meaning of interstate commerce to carry out executive and legislative policy during the 1930 depression. Yet, while blacks were lynched, the federal government was unable to interfere. Pointing to the state action or inaction in the different branches of state government is not a display of legal shadow boxing; the continuing responsibility of the different branches of government—the interplay between executive, legislative, and judicial authority—points to the emptiness of categorization. It further emphasizes that separation of function leads to buck-passing in the government. If a state legislature "passes the buck" to residents, as in *Reitman,* then it will also wait for another branch of government to deal with a painful problem. Black schoolteachers in the South were paid less than the white, with nary a sound from legislators, jurists, and members of the executive branch. The *amicus curiae* brief also points to the interrelationship between branches of government, blurring the traditional lines of distinction, at least in the civil rights cases.

The Fifth and Fourteenth Amendments are not the best strategic weapons to hit at discrimination, but they can be useful substitutes where direct means are unavailable; their value should not be overlooked when a political game is played with the black. The Fourteenth Amendment continues to serve a useful purpose where all "horses" are still needed to help the black. For example, unfair labor practice charges carry a six-month statute of limitations while the federal EEOC is hemmed in by ninety-day time limitation. The Fifth and Fourteenth Amendments can be used without a confining deadline.[272] Furthermore, sociological data may be more pertinent in a Fourteenth Amendment case than one arising in a federal district court under Title VII of the Civil Rights Act of 1964. A finding of a violation of the Fifth or Fourteenth Amendment hits at general government practices, calling for widespread correction. The impact of a decision under a fair employment law typically touches the participants to the suit without reaching into other corners. In such a situation, the use of the Fifth or Fourteenth Amendment has greater impact.

Reaching prejudice in the courtroom is costly, time-consuming, and the "wholesale" aspects of discrimination are too frequently untouched.[273] Although the doctrine of state action may be needed less frequently in the future, it will remain useful to combat discrimination.

CHAPTER SIX ⁑ ECONOMIC CONDITIONS: 1960 TO PRESENT

While legislative and other procedures slowly bring about changes, there are obvious links of weakness that delay fair employment. These weaknesses will now be explored, looking at conditions as they currently exist, including current legislation, procedural operation, and alternatives.

The economic status of blacks in the United States has been well documented in recent years.[274] It is well known that, by any accepted measure of economic welfare, the average black does not fare as well as the average white.

The unemployment rate for blacks is twice that for whites (see Table 1). In fact, it is higher for nonwhite high school graduates than for white high school dropouts. Furthermore, the labor force participation rate for nonwhites has been declining, but it has been stable for whites. Slightly more than one-half of all nonwhite males who worked in 1964 had fulltime year-round jobs compared with two-thirds of all white males.[275]

Average income is lower for blacks. For farm families in 1964, the median income for blacks was one-half that of whites. For nonfarm families, the black median income was three-fifths the white median income.

Blacks with equivalent jobs or educations have lower incomes than their white counterparts. A larger proportion of nonwhite than white male high school graduates hold blue-collar jobs.[276]

At every income level, a higher percentage of blacks than whites live in substandard housing. Black families are about half as likely to be home-owners as white families. They pay higher interest rates if they are home-owners. They must buy a previously occupied house rather than a new one much more frequently than white families because of the unavailability of mortgage money and price. And nonwhites pay more than the estimated value of the house twice as often as whites.

Forty per cent of all nonwhite children live in overcrowded housing or housing lacking some facilities. Nonwhite substandard housing increased greatly in proportion to all housing units between 1950 and 1960, while the relative number of nonwhite households scarcely changed. The pattern of segregated housing continues. More than one-half of the urban blacks live in tracts in which over 90 per cent of the population is black.[277]

Nonwhite death rates remain strikingly higher than white death rates.

Table 1
Selected Unemployment Rates for 1954, 1958, 1961, 1964, 1968

Unemployment Rate

Year	All Workers	White	Non-white	White Male 18-19 yrs	Nonwhite Male 18-19 yrs
1954	5.5	5.0	9.9	13.0	14.7
1958	6.8	6.1	12.6	16.5	26.7
1961	6.7	6.0	12.4	15.1	23.9
1964	5.2	4.6	9.6	13.4	23.1
1968	3.6	3.2	6.7	8.2	19.0

Sources: *Manpower Report of the President 1968*, 237. *Annual Report of the Council of Economic Advisers* 1969, 255. U.S. Department of Labor, Bureau of Labor Statistics, *Employment and Earnings and Monthly Report on the Labor Force,* Vol. 15, January, 1969, p. 113.

Life expectancy at all ages is lower for nonwhites. The gap between white and nonwhite infant and maternal mortality is widening.[278]

The median education level for blacks is lower than that of whites. Currently, school enrollment rates are about the same for white and black between the ages of 7 and 17. However, they are much lower for nonwhites in their kindergarten and college years. There is also no doubt that the quality of education, received or being received, for most blacks is below that for most whites.[279]

Have blacks in the United States progressed? How rapidly are they improving their economic status, and how does this compare with whites? In attempting to answer these questions, it is customary to compare black attainment today with the level of black attainment at some other time or to compare black-white differentials today with black-white differentials at some other time. The first type of comparison usually shows improvement, but it says nothing about the status of blacks relative to that of whites. The second type of comparison is more meaningful because it does take this into account. However, it is often difficult to interpret. Sometimes the absolute differences between white and nonwhite indicators behave differently than do the ratios of the same indicators.

Fein uses the following example to illustrate this difficulty. In 1940, the absolute difference between white and nonwhite infant mortality rates was 31 per 1,000 live births, while in 1962 the difference had declined to 19 per 1,000. Yet in 1940 the nonwhite infant mortality rate was 70 per cent greater than that of whites, and in 1962 it was 91 per cent greater.[280]

Has the relative status of the black to the white improved with respect to infant mortality since 1940? Well, yes and no. It is obvious from this ex-

78

ample that a narrowing differential does not necessarily mean that the gap between white and black is being closed. Furthermore, a narrowing differential fails to show that frequently the black is moving up more slowly than the white did in the past.

Fein has used this type of comparison—a time-lag statistic—in assessing the relative status of whites and blacks.[281] This statistic measures how many years earlier the white American attained the particular level of income, education, etc., that the black has achieved today to show whether the gap (in years) is greater or less than in earlier periods. This provides a comparison of the relative speed of movement over the same range of experience. The change in the length of the gap depends upon the relative rates of change of white and black indicators over time. The results of such a comparison are very discouraging. In many instances, the time gap has been widening rather than narrowing. Today, the black is further behind the white (in years) than he once was. Several examples are given below.

In 1962, the life expectancy of blacks was about six years less than for whites. It was also approximately the same as that for whites in 1940. However, the rate of progress up to this life expectancy was the same for both races. It took 40 years (1900 to 1940) for the white life expectancy to rise from 48 to 62, and it took 40 years (1920 to 1960) for the black life expectancy to go from 48 to 62. However, we would have expected the black to move more rapidly. He represents approximately 10 per cent of the population, and the knowledge which had permitted the white to progress was already there; he did not have to wait for the next scientific advance as did the white.

The time-lag statistics concerning education, infant mortality, and income are even more disheartening. The black's status, while improving, is not improving as rapidly as that of the white when he was at the same economic level.[282]

It is still too early to tell what effect the programs of the 1960s in manpower, human capital, etc., have had. Hopefully they are reversing this trend, but we cannot be sure.

Another way of indicating the inferior economic status of blacks is to look at their loss of income due to underemployment. This in turn can be divided into short-run and long-run effect.

Today, one reason for the low median income for blacks is that they are underemployed. The existing skills of blacks are not being utilized to their full potential. The underemployment can be divided into four categories:

1) Unemployment: It has been mentioned earlier that the black unemployment ratio is about twice that for whites.
2) Part-time work: A much higher percentage of blacks than whites is only able to find part-time work.[283]

3) Nonskilled jobs for skilled workers: many blacks cannot find jobs which utilize their skills.

4) Low labor force participation rates: Because of the above three factors, many blacks do not seek work.[284]

Accordingly, the official unemployment statistics understate the real amount of underemployment among blacks.

It has been estimated that if the black unemployment rate were as low as that for whites, total black income would rise by about $1.5 billion.[285] We estimate that black income would rise by an additional $1.3 billion if all aspects of black underemployment were reduced to the same rate as that for whites. In total, the higher underemployment of blacks reduces their income by $2.8 billion.

However, this $2.8 billion represents only part of the loss to society due to the underemployment of blacks. If the underemployment were reduced to the rate for whites, the additional earned income of $2.8 billion would lead to additional increases in national income. Most of the $2.8 billion would be spent, leading to an increase in aggregate demand which would generate further income increases. Through the working of the Keynesian multiplier, the total increase in annual income in the United States would be between 10 and 15 billion dollars. Given the present inflationary situation, some of this increase would be eaten up by price increases. However, a substantial percentage of the 10 and 15 billion dollars would be a gain in real income, some of which would go to whites. Thus, not only are blacks being hurt by underemployment, but the white is also economically injured.

The long-run losses in national income due to underemployment of blacks are even more substantial. The percentage of blacks prevented from developing their potential due to inferior education, malnutrition, inadequate medical care, and other forms of cultural deprivation is considerably higher than for whites. Therefore, even if the types of short-run underemployment discussed above were eliminated, the average income of blacks would be below that of whites.

How much higher would black income be if he developed the same skills as the average white and the short-run underemployment rates were equal? This is an extremely difficult question to answer because wage rates and wage differentials would be restructured if this happy situation were to exist. However, we would submit as a very rough approximation an increase of 15 billion dollars. This again is only the first stage; the total effect on national income would probably be two or three times this figure.

The Keynesian Revolution resulted in the federal government's assuming responsibility for stabilizing aggregate economic activity. The results have been relatively successful, if judged against the past. However, it is obvious that the results have been far from perfect. During the 1950s, economic growth in the United States lagged behind that of other industrial countries, prices rose, there were numerous recessions with increasingly high levels of unemployment, and the unemployment rate for blacks remained distressingly high.

Most of the poor economic performance by the United States can be attributed to the monetary and fiscal policies of the 1950s. Unfortunately, President Eisenhower and some of his advisers were not sufficiently keyed to Keynesian thinking, and his administration failed to take the action necessary to maintain a high level of employment. The Federal Reserve Board also demonstrated a penchant for ill-timed changes in monetary policy, which contributed to the string of recessions characteristic of this period.

As recessions became increasingly frequent and recoveries increasingly less satisfactory, the concept of structural unemployment gained followers. In each period of recovery, the unemployment rate remained higher than it had been in the previous recovery period. The unemployment rates for several classifications within the labor force, especially nonwhites and teenagers, were much higher than the average unemployment rate. And the gap widened during these years. Table 1 illustrates the unemployment rates by classification for 1954, 1958, and 1961, the worst years of three recessions.

These factors led many to believe that the number of structurally unemployed was increasing, i.e., that the number of individuals without the necessary skill to be gainfully employed was increasing due to technological and industrial changes. Those accepting this view argued that increases in aggregate demand would not significantly effect the unemployment rate. This view was not accepted by all economists, and many argued that the problem was primarily insufficient aggregate demand.

This argument has never been fully resolved, but the structural hypothesis has fallen into disfavor. Most economists believe that the experience of the 1960s demonstrates that high levels of aggregate demand can bring about lower unemployment rates.

The argument over structural employment did highlight some of the shortcomings of the accepted economic theory of the early 1950s. Awareness of these shortcomings during the late 1950s and 1960s led to new concepts in public policy. The people hurt most by the unemployment of the 1950s, as in any other period, were those with the least skill, especially the black. The unemployed and underemployed in the United States are largely those who have not developed their potential or been given an opportunity to develop skills leading to steady, high paying jobs. Maintaining sufficient aggregate demand is one necessary step in solving this problem; *government action makes the job available*. The other necessary step is to insure

81

to all citizens the opportunity to develop the skills necessary to fill high paying jobs.

The impact of investment on aggregate economic activity has always been stressed by Keynesian economists. However, until recently, almost all discussion of investment was limited to investment in *physical* capital. The need and desirability of investing money in people in order to increase their productivity was overlooked. Investment in education, training programs, medical care, and housing to improve the quality of *human* capital is as necessary for economic growth as are new factories, highways, etc. Many economists have devoted their efforts in recent years to investigating and demonstrating the importance of investment in human capital. A number of federal programs in these areas, later discussed, have been initiated since 1960. Since black Americans have not received their share of investment in human capital, i.e., they have been shortchanged in education, medical care, etc., they are among the prime beneficiaries of federal investment in human capital.

A high level of aggregate demand and a well-trained labor force do not insure perfectly functioning labor markets or the absolute minimum level of unemployment. Ignorance of job opportunities or discrimination by employers and unions have been major causes of higher than necessary unemployment rates in the United States. In recent years, legislation to alleviate both conditions, later discussed, has been passed.

A high level of aggregate demand, a well-trained labor force, properly functioning labor markets, knowledge of job opportunities, and elimination of discrimination will still leave unemployment and families with inadequate incomes. As long as the market system is the institution through which wages and salaries are determined, some individuals will be unable to earn a living wage. In a market system, men and women are theoretically paid according to their productivity (unions, admittedly, have introduced an important change). This is roughly the case in the United States, although there are many exceptions. However, eliminating all imperfections in the market would not eliminate the unpleasant fact that some individuals are not productive or that some individuals cannot be expected to neglect other responsibilities to increase their income. The aged, the disabled, and the uneducated cannot be expected to earn a decent wage. As another example, society may be better off in the long run if mothers with dependent children are not forced to leave their children to go to work.

Society has always realized that some people require financial assistance; charity and public welfare are the typical responses. However, there has always been a stigma attached to those receiving a dole. Some people feel that those receiving public or private charity are less honorable and less desirable citizens. The percentage of blacks on dole has been higher than whites due to inferior education, discrimination in employment and wages, union discrimination, etc.

In recent years, an increasing number of people have realized that our system of income maintenance for those unable to support themselves is grossly inadequate and an affront to personal dignity. In an affluent society, no one should live in poverty. If an individual cannot earn an adequate income, support should come from the government in a manner which, as far as possible, is neither degrading nor a sign of second-class citizenship. A guaranteed annual income has been proposed in place of the charitable dole. A proposal for a guaranteed income currently receiving considerable attention is the negative income tax.

In addition to removing the charitable stigma, a negative income tax would lead to a tax structure more symmetrical than the existing one. The current system of income tax permits each family to deduct a certain amount, based upon the number of dependents and selected expenses, from his gross income. If the residual or net income is greater than zero, the family's income tax is a specified per cent of net income. If the net income is zero, the income tax is zero. However, if the net income is negative (i.e., deductions are greater than gross income), the income tax is still zero. The proposal for a negative income tax would make the income tax in the last instance a negative amount. In other words, instead of an income tax equal to zero, the federal government would give money to the family.

One proposal for a negative income tax calls for a tax of zero for a family of four when annual family income is $4,800.[286] For every three dollars below $4,800, the family would receive one dollar from the government. Put another way, if income were zero, the family would receive $1,600. For every three dollars earned, the government payment would be reduced by one dollar until family income reached $4,800, when government support would end.

The negative income tax has three main advantages over existing welfare programs. First, it provides income as a matter of right, without a test of need or other degrading aspects of current welfare. The second is that incentives to work are provided for those physically able. The negative income tax enables an individual to keep a substantial share of any money that he earns; he keeps two-thirds of his earnings, while receiving the negative income tax previously discussed. Most welfare programs reduce payment by the amount a person earns—in effect a 100 per cent tax—substantially reducing the incentive to leave the welfare roles and work for a living. The third advantage is that it should be less expensive to administer. For example, it will reduce the amount of time social workers spend investigating the financial status of the recipient, freeing them for more valuable work.

The negative income tax is one way of providing a guaranteed annual income. Another method is simply to give everybody a certain amount per year without reduction even though income rises. Another method is to guarantee a job to everyone, a right guaranteed in the Russian Constitution, and thus provide a guaranteed annual *wage*. The major difficulty with this approach is that some people cannot be expected to work and additional provision would have to be made to care for them. The major difficulty with the negative income tax or any guaranteed income is that if the guaranteed income is above the poverty level and sufficient additional income is kept to provide adequate work incentive, substantial payments are made to families above the poverty level. Perhaps some compromise between a negative income tax and existing welfare programs can be devised.

Of more importance to this discussion than the details of any specific income maintenance program is the economist's growing concern with income distribution. Economists have set forth a variety of plans to assist those at the lower end of this distribution. Whatever method is used, it is clear that improvement in our income maintenance programs will greatly aid the black community, because such a high percentage fall below the poverty line.

CHAPTER SEVEN ✖ ABILITY AND PERSONALITY TESTS

The Catalyst

Since 1963, employers have placed increasing reliance on tests to select and promote employees.[287] With the decision in the *Motorola*[288] fiasco, Congress, considering the passage of fair employment legislation, became concerned with protecting the employer using a test, and the black was ignored. Because of the publicity and notoriety surrounding the *Motorola* case, issues were sufficiently clouded and public sentiment gathered to protect employers using tests.[289]

Unions have gone to arbitration to question the right of employers to use tests without contesting their validity and reliability, with arbitrators unwilling to outlaw testing.[290] If arbitrators had been presented with evidence of employer failure to validate and check reliability, some testing could have been stopped.[291] But unions also rely on tests for membership, unchecked for "scientific" accuracy, and the pot could not point to the blackening of the kettle.

The *Motorola* case is quixotic. A black trained to service radio and television receivers applied for a job at the Motorola plant in Chicago. The applicant was informed that he would not be hired because he failed a written test. A complaint of employment discrimination was made to the Illinois Fair Employment Practice Commission which investigated and found evidence to substantiate the complaint. The Motorola Corporation refused to participate in the conciliation process conducted by the Illinois Commission because a stenographer was not permitted.[292] A public hearing was held, and the hearing officer ordered Motorola to hire the complainant. On review, the Illinois Commission also found evidence of discrimination; however, it was decided that the complainant was not entitled to a job, and he was awarded $1,000 in damages. On appeal to the Chicago Circuit Court, it was decided that the Commission was not legislatively authorized to award damages while upholding the decision that the employer had discriminated.

While agreeing with the decision that the Motorola Corporation was guilty of intentional discrimination, the complainant was stripped of any remedy by the Illinois Commission and Chicago Circuit Court.

The Illinois Supreme Court reversed in favor of the employer, because the hearing examiner and Commission did not follow the legal rules of evidence. The Court said:

> When all the evidence in this case is considered, some suspicion might remain that the plaintiff (Motorola) has falsely recorded (the complainant's) test score. Under the . . . Act, however, that suspicion is not enough. The Act provides that "(a) determination sustaining a complaint shall be based upon a preponderance of the evidence." On the record in this case, we are of the opinion that the alleged unfair employment practice was not established by a preponderance of the evidence.[293]

Under Illinois law, legal rules of evidence must be followed; most state commissions are not required to establish wrongdoing by a preponderance of evidence although some evidence is necessary.[294]

An interesting facet of the decision by the Illinois hearing examiner was the view that the firm has . . .

> a supreme responsibility to move positively to eradicate unfair employment practices in every department. . . . The employer may have to establish in-plant training programs and employ the heretofore culturally deprived and disadvantaged persons as learners, placing them under such supervision that will *enable* them to achieve job success.[295]

In addition, the trial examiner said that he orally administered the test to the complainant who passed it.[296] Consequently, the employer, who could not produce or would not produce evidence that the test was failed, discriminated.

The inspiration for Section 703 (h) of the Civil Rights Act, which protects the employer relying on "the professionally developed ability test," was the stand taken by the Illinois hearing examiner that testing blacks was inherently discriminatory. Since he had already decided that the complainant passed the Motorola test, all testing was unfortunately spotlighted by the dictum. Cases reaching the court prior to *Motorola* had not indicated that testing was inherently discriminatory.[297] To fan the public fire, the Illinois Commission did not find the test inherently discriminatory.

There is currently more criticism of industrial testing than ever before. Yet, employers rely more frequently on tests than in the past. If the public goal of fair employment is to be realized, the judiciary must take a closer look at sociological, psychological, and other evidence casting considerable doubt on the propriety of testing in general.

General Commentary

Irrespective of the professional status and integrity of the person responsible for its preparation, the test is not an infallible method of employee selection, and many are unfair to the black. In fact, some critics take the position that every test is discriminatory, inevitably reaching into the past of those tested rather than ferreting out ability to handle a job. While a test less discriminatory than others can be devised—this is more difficult to accomplish than generally conceded—too many put into use damage the quest for fair employment. Perhaps the ill-advised reliance on tests could be ignored if the economic, educational, and social gap between black and white were being closed rapidly or employers and unions were convinced that fair employment must be achieved quickly. The little progress made in narrowing the economic disparity between white and black has taken considerable time and effort. Unless the executive and judicial branches of government take more powerful swings at controlling the use of the test, it may be the most effective method devised to retard fair employment. The entire Civil Rights Act of 1964 is a political grab bag in which the hand of compromise is everywhere seen. There is considerable evidence that many in Congress were less concerned with fair employment than was indicated by the vote in favor of the Civil Rights Act of 1964. To "entice" congressional approval, Section 703 (h) was put into the package without considering what several hundred years of discrimination had done to the black. Make no mistake—many members of Congress did not sympathize with those in greatest need of sympathy.

Fair employment laws, all of them, are unfortunately, geared to achieving results in the long run while the black is entitled to an immediate breakthrough. If justice is the goal, the executive branch of government and courts will have to "carry the ball." The executive orders, if diligently enforced, are geared to realize immediate improvement. To assure fair employment now, the Department of Labor has issued a directive, later discussed, aimed at unfair testing. The judiciary must also show greater ingenuity to "grease" the way for immediate progress.

An ideal test is one in which white and black perform equally well, sifting out those without the necessary aptitude to perform the job. Unfortunately, this ideal is difficult if not impossible to realize and even the well-prepared test does not guarantee the selection of the qualified. For this reason, employers rely on other selective techniques to assure the hiring of the best job candidate. In fact, the employer relying exclusively on tests must be looked at closely to detect a discriminatory motive.

Blacks do not perform as well on tests as whites. Children moving to Harlem from the South register lower scores on intelligence tests than black children raised in the North. During World War I, northern blacks scored higher on tests administered by the Army than southern blacks.[298] Those in the lower socioeconomic strata tend to perform less satisfactorily on tests than those coming from the white middle class.[299] Foreign applicants seeking admission to a graduate school perform poorly on entrance tests when compared to the white citizen of the United States.[300]

The less satisfactory performance on tests by the black can be attributed to a language barrier, the same reasons that the foreigner performs poorly on tests—an unfamiliarity with the language used by middle-class America and considerably less background in the subject matter tested.[301] The southern black has not scored as well as the northern black because of an even greater language barrier. The black living in the isolated ghetto or rural South has limited contact with the outside world and suffers on tests because of a language barrier and inferior schooling.[302] Test scores too often reflect the social structure of our society rather than reaching for those with ability to hold a job.[303]

Many reasons can be assigned to deemphasize test scores to select employees. As already indicated, a satisfactory score on a test is only one indicator of minimal ability.[304] Personnel managers know, or should know, that exclusive reliance on one method of selection increases the probability of placement error and that black scores will be low. Yet, black job applicants coached to take a test fare better than white applicants who are unprepared. But the candidate failing to prepare for the test who scores poorly is not necessarily inferior.[305] Drawing a line between a passing and failing score forces an arbitrary decision. A score slightly below the cutoff point does not necessarily point to a prospect less satisfactory than someone passing the test. There is nothing scientific about picking a cutoff point; anyone in academia is aware of this limitation.[306] Cutoff scores are often geared to the supply of labor and the number of positions to be filled rather than the minimal ability considered satisfactory. An employer who refuses to employ a black narrowly missing a passing score must be viewed suspiciously if other selective devices are not restorted to. Blacks have been tutored in a few days by the Workers Defense League, a black organization in New York City, to pass tests.[307] If people can be tutored in a few days to pass a test, the whole concept of testing to select employees is questionable. Furthermore, stress, sleep, noise, or an extremely warm or cold testing center can affect the score.

The motivation, speed, and attitude of the person taking a test are factors affecting the score. When the Supreme Court in *Plessy v. Ferguson* decreed that separate but equal facilities was constitutionally acceptable and discrimination by private employers was given a green light in the *Civil Rights Cases*, the motivation, speed, and attitude of the black was almost as much retarded as in slavery. Deny opportunity for gainful and equal employment and the desire to excel in the classroom and elsewhere will disappear. It is impossible to measure the incalculable damage of discrimination to black motivation and ego, which affects his score on a test.[308]

The Judicial Problem

Before a test can be psychologically nondiscriminatory for black and white, the following factors are important:

1. Exposure to similar cultural and educational opportunities.
2. The incentive to excel must be essentially equal.

Unfortunately, the judge weighing the discriminatory nature of a test deals with conditions that the employer did not create—all of society is responsible for the black hangup. Can an employer be held legally responsible for that which he did not individually create? Probably not, but the judge interested in fair employment is not without legal tools to force the employer to shoulder some of the responsibility if sociological and psychological evidence is considered.

A test is improperly developed unless these educational guidelines are followed:

1. The test must be related to job specifications.
2. The test must be validated and its reliability reviewed periodically.[309] The sample should be checked when a test is validated to assure its adequacy.
3. The test must be administered in good faith and without discrimination.[310]

Ascertaining the relation of the test to job specifications, validation and reliability are relatively simple judicial tasks to watch over, but good faith, or the lack thereof, presents a more difficult evidentiary problem. Good faith and intent are wrapped in the same bundle. Intent in the courtroom is traditionally established by what is done and not a failure to act. In *Wilmington*, state inaction was equated with state action, if on government property, to find a violation of the Fourteenth Amendment, but nonaction by the private employer is not yet treated as a sign of discrimination.

The "Professionally Developed" Test

Section 703 (h) states:

(N)or shall it be an unlawful employment practice for an employer to give and act upon the result of any professionally developed ability test provided that such test, its administration or action upon the results is not designed, intended, or used to discriminate because of race. . . .

Section 703 (h) calls for a "professionally developed" test. The employer using a test that is not "professionally developed" is presumably not protected by Section 703 (h), and violates Section 703 (a), an unfair employment practice. The Civil Rights Act does not define "professionally developed," a task that must be undertaken by the EEOC and judiciary. It is important that the judge look to the criteria established by those deemed to be professionals. That Congress pointed to "professionally developed" as a criterion means that care must be exercised by the judiciary before endorsing the use of a test. There is no question but that psychologists and educators, professionals, find many tests unacceptable.

The EEOC is without authority to hold an employer responsible for discrimination. While the EEOC can investigate and conciliate, its decision cannot be enforced in court. Employers are aware of this limitation and a failure to tailor the test to job specifications, validate, and review reliability are more than indiscretions, more than nonaction by the firm. The failure to follow professional standards is often a blatant, deliberate disregard of the legislative call for "professionally developed." To permit the employer to escape responsibility for using the test that does not follow professional guidelines ignores the congressional mandate.

The court looking at a test under Section 703 (h) has a number of alternatives. The judge could rule that Section 703 (h) only outlaws intentional discrimination, which must be established by evidence other than a failure to follow professional guidelines. A judge could also rule that the failure to follow professional guidelines is a *per se* violation. Another alternative is to shift the burden of proof to the employer to show that he did not discriminate. Whatever Congress intended under the umbrella of the "professionally developed" test, the EEOC and courts have wide latitude to fix standards to protect the black well within the arsenal of acceptable legal tactics.

A mystery of life is the meaning of "professionally developed." Since legislative guidance is sparse, including the congressional hearings, it must be concluded that Congress delegated to the EEOC and courts responsibility for establishing professional standards. The concept of "professionally developed" seems to embrace two separate notions—the making of a test, including a hard look at what the test is supposed to do, and the background of the individual preparing the test. Fitting the test to job specifications, validation, and reliability match the "nuts and bolts" that go into the preparation of a test.

The EEOC *Guidelines*[311] refer to *Standards for Educational and Psychological Tests and Manuals*,[312] which describes the desirable testing methodology. These references indicate that the EEOC is primarily concerned with the means used to hammer a test together rather than the professional background of its creator. Where competency and professionalism are important, training and background are difficult to separate from the

90

finished product in spite of the fact that amateurs succeed. Succinctly, a "professionally developed" test is synonymous with the "professionally" trained person. But Section 703 (h) only mentions "professionally developed," without referring to the background of the one preparing the test. Unless background is read into "professionally developed," the employer unconcerned with the qualifications of the person preparing the test is home free.

Standards have not been established to evaluate the qualification of the test designer. In law and medicine, completion of a professional school and the passing of a state board, usually rigorous, are required. But in psychology and education, the two fields of educational specialization that have preempted the testing market, qualifications have not been standardized, except in academia where the door-opener is the doctor of philosophy. Some consulting firms preparing tests are staffed by employees meeting the standards of academia. Academicians "moonlight" and prepare tests for industry. Some consultants, however, do not meet the artificial standard of academia even though competent. University professors preparing tests for industry hardly qualify as professionals after looking at some of their finished products. Should a "professionally" qualified tester be certified by a state board? Would a Ph.D. in psychology, education, or any other discipline suffice? Could the holder of a bachelor's or master's degree, particularly if experienced, satisfy a standard of professionalism?

An employer could ask an employee to prepare a test. The house man, irrespective of his professional competence, is expected to display "loyalty" to the firm; and the employer unwilling to make an effort to assure equal employment opportunity "signals" that the test will be used to keep blacks out. Not that it is difficult to hire a consultant to design a discriminatory test. But from the judicial perspective, should the house-prepared test be viewed more suspiciously than one prepared by the consultant? Our answer is a qualified and tongue-in-cheek "yes" because the label "professional" is an empty designation when working for industry. Nevertheless, Section 703 (h) does not, and probably should not, expressly exclude an employee from the professional class.

The EEOC has decided that a test should be "devised by a person or firm in the business or profession of developing tests, but, in addition, the tests must be developed and applied in accordance with the accepted standards of testing performance."[313] However, the exclusion of the house man as professionally qualified is not authoritative since the EEOC is not authorized to make a binding decision. If the EEOC and courts looked at the qualifications of the employee preparing the test and insisted upon the following of job specifications, validation, and reliability, there would be less need to exclude automatically the test prepared by the house man.

Turning to the "scientific" steps, the *Standards for Educational and Psychological Tests and Manuals* calls for the validation of all tests. The EEOC *Guidelines* also provide that "(o)nly a test which has been validated for minorities can be assumed to be free of inadvertent bias."[314] Based on these two professionally prepared manuals, an unvalidated test does not qualify as "professionally developed." Tests administered by employers are often unvalidated or validated for one plant or geographic area and used elsewhere. Stock tests are often bought by employers without ascertaining validity.

The employer relying on an unvalidated test for employee selection is actually or constructively aware that the results are unreliable. Employees trained in personnel administration are aware that the test result cannot be accepted at face value. Based on the evidence of widespread discrimination and the inability of the black to progress economically, the employer using an unvalidated test can be treated as a *per se* violator. While Section 703 (h) protects the employer administering or accepting "the results" of a test "not designed, intended, or used to discriminate," the failure to validate has to be taken as evidence of wrongdoing. Due to the adverse publicity given tests in recent years and the suggestions in *Standards and Guidelines*, the failure to validate, an omission, is proper evidence of discrimination. This point will be considered again when shifting the burden of proof is discussed.

The Department of Labor since 1965 is charged with administering Executive Order 11246, overseeing the letting of government contracts requiring fair employment. The Department of Labor has issued a directive to all federal agencies that "each contractor regularly using tests" must submit "evidence that the tests are valid for their intended purposes."[315] The directive further states that "(u)nder no circumstances will the general reputation of a test, its author or its publisher, or casual reports of test utility be accepted in lieu of evidence of validity."[316] It differs from the EEOC *Guidelines* which urge but do not require validation. (However, even if the *Guidelines* were mandatory, the EEOC is without enforcement power.) The directive from the Department of Labor does not state that a failure to validate automatically results in the cancellation of a government contract or results in the imposition of another penalty on the employer.

The Personality Test

Psychologists do not simply define "personality," and the term does not imply positive or negative qualities. Personality tests used in industry are in a primitive state, drawing upon a few characteristics chosen by the tester to highlight desirable or nondesirable attributes.[317] Personality testing fits into two categories—type theories in which people are fitted into common categories, like bookworms, conservatives, extroverts, etc.; and trait theories, which show differences between people.[318] Most personality tests used by industry fall into the trait type and are of the pencil and paper variety (rather than observation).

The task of the psychologist is to identify observable traits. The tester then decides which traits are desirable or nondesirable in the employee. The employer selecting desirable and undesirable traits all too often ignores the basic question, the ability of the testee to perform the job. Further, the value of personality testing is doubtful because of the absence of validity and reliability. The validity of the personality test is difficult to establish since the accuracy and relevancy of the test is doubtful in the first instance. The reliability of the test is doubtful because people change and the assumption is false that retaking a test measures the same thing.[319]

Section 703 (h) mentions only the "ability test," a test designed to uncover learning capacity, performing capability, industrial judgment, etc. Since other test categories are unnamed and Section 703 (h) followed in the wake of the initial *Motorola* decision, which condemned generally the ability test, the question arises of whether Congress extended the same protection to the personality test. Whatever underlying support may be extended to justify the use of the ability test cannot be carried over to the personality test. Employers testing to determine morality, social presence, social views, character, emotional stability, etc., should not be protected by Section 703 (h). The directive issued by the Department of Labor covering government contracts lumps together the intelligence and ability test as well as the "personality or temperament" test. While an intelligence test may be part of the arsenal necessary to uncover ability, the personality test seldom relates to ability. An interesting question is raised: what standards should be used to judge the validity of the personality test if it is assumed that professionalism, as previously discussed, is necessary?

Since Section 703 (h) saves the "ability test," the use of a personality test could be considered prima facie evidence of discrimination while government contracts controlled by Executive Order 11246 permit the validated personality test. If judicially determined that Congress intended only to protect the "ability test," the executive order protecting the personality test is out of order, contrary to congressional will. Personal freedom and the welfare of the black are at stake where the personality test is used. Among psychologists there is no one accepted theory of personality; there is a variety of theories that overlap. The drafter of a personality test for industry has a model in mind of acceptable behavior and ideology, a model that will not "rock the boat." Job applicants burning with revolutionary spirit, those finding society morally weak, and those raised in the black ghetto will frequently fail to match the conceptual model of the drafter.

93

Moral and social views are infrequently related to performance on the job, leading to an inference that the employer engaging in personality testing intends to discriminate. While fair employment is a goal legislatively expressed, the legislative compromises and action by members of Congress hardly point to a determined will to provide equality of economic opportunity. The employer knows that society is not firmly committed to racial equality and the unchecked use of the personality test is a near perfect weapon to continue patterns of the past. The courts, executive agencies, and the EEOC, to further the goal of fair employment, must appreciate the lethal aspects of the personality test. Particularly when the black successfully completes an aptitude test but fails a personality test is there evidence of impropriety.[320]

Most employers turn to the ability and personality test to make the initial selection of the employee.[321] The personality of an employee, particularly one whose merit rating indicates average ability or better and in the absence of unusual circumstances, does not need a going-over to determine his suitability for a better job. The personality of the jobholder is known to his immediate superiors and fellow workers. Furthermore, personality is often reflected in his merit rating; on-the-job performance and personality are difficult to separate. Jobs in the blue-collar category and lower-level management can be filled without personality tests, and many middle- and high-level management positions could be manned without reaching into skeletal corners, too often an unjustified invasion of privacy.

Where there is a history of actual or sociological discrimination, the employer currently initiating a policy calling for the use of the ability or personality test acts suspiciously. One firm guilty of past discrimination decided for the first time in 1964 to test employees for promotion. Fifty-eight per cent of the white employees tested passed while only one out of seventeen blacks succeeded.[322] While federal courts have been told by Congress to ignore past discrimination, testing for promotion since 1963 is a sign calling for judicial care and represents some evidence of a continuation of past policy.

Justice Brandeis in 1928 felt that citizens are entitled to be protected "in their beliefs, their thoughts, their emotions, and their sensations."[323] Tests have been administered for reasons other than a search for skill and aptitude, tests that reach into hidden corners of character, and religious, social, political, and sexual attitudes.[324] To permit employers to reach into hidden corners of the lives of employees is dangerous to the person, society, and industry. The same outlook on life may lead to a "safe" environment, but it certainly is not a creative or challenging one. Academicians and critics of our current society challenge the right of an employer to hold onto a social code and mores reminiscent of the nineteenth and early twentieth century while resorting elsewhere to modern technical devices. Psychologists have hardly scratched the surface of personality, and the employer willing to rely on the personality test hardly matches the concept of the scientifically oriented entrepreneur.

The personality test is a deterrent to fair employment. These tests show that the black does not fit the slot assigned to the middle-class white. These tests are used to show that critics of our society are not to share industry bounty. While the Fourth and Fifth Amendments protect somewhat the individual from mental search by government, these safeguards, unfortunately, do not place a rein on the employer. The ghetto black can be downgraded for personality traits considered undesirable by industry.[325] While the ghetto black was once interested in emulating the successful "whitey," many today tear down white values, building black morale and ego. It is absolutely essential for peaceful coexistence that the black community does its thing in its own way, if for no other reason than therapeutic value. Taking a stand now will also help the white who truly practices individuality.

Ignoring whether a personality test is proper, at the very least a competent and reliable psychologist should prepare and evaluate the test. As Section 703 (h) calls for the "professionally developed" test, only a qualified psychologist—perhaps one with a doctorate and experience—should prepare it. While Section 703 (h) mentions only the "professionally developed" test, to assess fairly the results calls for the "professionally" trained interpreter. The research and academically oriented psychologist is aware that personality tests measure the values of those preparing them and conclusive interpretations are dangerous and meaningless. Since *Standards for Educational and Psychological Tests and Manuals* discusses only the preferred methodology of creating tests, it is not helpful. To prepare and interpret a personality test requires extensive training and experience in psychology. A court considering the personality test under Section 703 (h) should look at the two aspects of professionalism previously noted: proper methodology and the training of the developer. A third requirement should be added for the personality test: those evaluating it must be professionally qualified.

Different Standards

To provide fair employment and follow EEOC *Guidelines*, different tests or different standards for black and white are necessary. A suggestion has been made that "we are not only justified in using different standards for different subcultural groups, but we are obliged to do so if we are to achieve the ultimate criterion of successful placement."[326] In *Guidelines*, the EEOC, while not expressly advocating separate standards and tests, suggested that employers seek out blacks[327] and those with a substandard score should be retested.[328] The suggested retesting is partially due to the discriminatory nature of many tests.

Aware that few complaints reach the federal district court, the EEOC, while only empowered to conciliate, can pressure employers to do more than Section 703 (h) requires or a court would call for. Some firms fearing the adverse publicity of a public suit and a black boycott are willing to settle "out of court" when privately pressured.

Whether the *Guidelines* and suggestions made for separate testing of black and white violate Title VII is at present speculative. At first blush, hunting for black employees, retesting failures, and allowing dual standards for black and white smack of reverse discrimination. These suggestions are made to benefit the black, a sign to some that employment preference over the white is intended. Section 703 (j) protects the employer unwilling to grant special concessions and coercion is forbidden. However Section 703 (j) does not forbid the employer to adopt voluntarily a policy giving some preference or advantage to the black. But Section 703 (a) (1) outlaws reverse discrimination even if voluntary. If *Guidelines* demands more of the employer than Congress, a court could strike out the EEOC and other suggestions. In our view, the suggestions in *Guidelines* and separate testing are an attempt to assure fair hiring by eliminating cultural factors. The elimination of factors unrelated to the ability to learn or job performance is no more than validation and a sign of being "professionally developed."

In our opinion, Congress, overwrought by the pending passage of the Civil Rights Act after more than twenty years of avoiding it and bowing to the newspaper hullabaloo surrounding the *Motorola* case, did not adequately weigh the consequences of Section 703 (h). Unless viewed imaginatively within the framework of the legal process, Section 703 (h) handicaps fair employment.

The Intent to Discriminate

There is some sentiment to show that Congress did not intend accidental or unintentional discrimination as evidence of a violation.[329] The "professionally developed ability test" was protected unless "designed, intended, or used to discriminate." Section 706 (g) authorized the federal district court to fashion appropriate relief if "the respondent has intentionally engaged in or is intentionally engaging in an unlawful employment practice. . . ."[330] Both Sections 703 (h) and 706 (g) outlaw intentional discrimination; if a test is unintentionally discriminatory, presumably a violation has not occurred. Even though a test may not meet the concept of "professionally developed," the employer in court claims no intent to discriminate because white and black are given the same test. And the charging party has been assigned the burden of proving an intentional violation in court.

Intent, while a subjective phenomenon, is established in the courtroom by pointing to external factors.[331] The difficulty of establishing intent when the employer uses a test should not be underestimated.[332] Playing the bookmakers' odds, it should be easier to establish an intentional violation where there is evidence of past discrimination and testing is currently resorted to. A recent case coming from the federal district court in North Carolina illustrates the evidentiary problem.[333] Ignoring past discrimination, the court looked only at an intelligence test and the requirement of a high school diploma. The court with care pointed out that the 1964 law was aimed at current and not past discrimination; the employer required a high school diploma before 1964; and a general intelligence test is not forbidden even though Section 703 (h) names the "ability test" only. In addition, the court concluded that an employer is not required to use "only those employment tests which accurately measure the ability and skills required of a particular job. . . ."[334]

Unmentioned by the North Carolina court was that the test (for promotion) was used after 1964 and whether there was need to "scientifically" administer an intelligence test to employees on the job. The decision of the court can be quarreled with: if the employer discriminated in the past and the test does not "accurately measure . . . ability and skills," the timing and lack of validity point to current discrimination. An investigation undertaken in 1968 by the EEOC pinpoints the widespread discrimination in the power industry.[335] While industry-wide discrimination is not evidence of discrimination by the individual power company, it does point to the need to scrutinize more closely the recruitment and promotion techniques resorted to by the members of the industry. The North Carolina court should have looked more closely at the test and its inevitable implication.

The North Carolina court and the Illinois court in *Motorola* could have considered shifting the burden of proof to the employer to establish the professional quality of the test. When the testing employer does not follow the suggestions made in *Guidelines* and *Standards for Educational and Psychological Tests and Manuals,* good faith must be questioned, particularly where other techniques of selection are not resorted to. Since he controls or can control the manner in which the test is put together, validated, and given, shifting the burden of proof to the employer to show that the test is not discriminatory is not unduly burdensome and is fairer to the complainant. Arbitrators appear to favor a rule that places the burden of proving invalidity of a test upon the complainant, a procedure unnecessarily harsh.[336] If the burden of proof can be shifted in the courtroom, the arbitrator, less bound by technicality, can follow a similar approach.

The burden of proof has been shifted in the courtroom where a complainant necessarily experiences difficulty proving his claim and the defendant controls the circumstances leading to the suit. *Res ipsa loquitur,* shifting the burden of proof to the defendant to show an absence of negligence, is followed in tort cases.[337] The burden of proof has been shifted to an employer accused of violating the Sherman Act—where 90 per cent of the relevant market is controlled by the firm, the court looks to the employer to submit evidence that monopolistic dominance was not deliberately pursued.[338] In *NLRB v. Fleetwood Trailer Co.,*[339] the Supreme Court ruled that an employer refusing to reinstate strikers must prove that he did not intend to discriminate against union members in violation of the Taft-Hartley Act. In *NLRB v. Great Dane Trailers,*[340] the Supreme Court decided that an antiunion motive need not be established when employee rights are crucially affected—it's up to the employer to produce evidence of legitimate motivation. Testing is similar—where an employer, particularly one discriminating in the past, tests, he should present evidence of his motivation.

Different approaches are taken in the courtroom to decide whether the plaintiff or defendant has the burden of proof.[341] One approach is to place the burden of proof on the party controlling the "happening," like the employer who tests. It appears that the complainant is unfairly saddled with proving the discriminatory nature of a test when the employer completely dominates the "happening." If the EEOC were permitted to make a binding decision, placing the burden of proof on the complainant would be less onerous since the evidentiary rules of the courtroom would not have to be followed (unless the federal law was patterned after the Illinois FEPC law). Another important factor influencing the approach to burden of proof is public policy.[342] The Civil Rights Act, in spite of its drawbacks, calls for the elimination of discrimination in employment. If fair employment is the public goal and discrimination is difficult to prove, lightening the load seems commendable. Following the call for legalism that pervades the Civil Rights Act, shifting the burden of proof is sound and socially desirable.

CHAPTER EIGHT ✖ SENIORITY

Union membership and bargaining power grew with the passage of the Wagner Act in 1935.[343] Although powerful in a few industries and localities before the 1930 depression, in the main unions were insignificant. Unions did not represent employees in steel, rubber, aluminum, automobile, and other industries dominated by large employers. Only in construction, printing, and a few other industries were craft unions powerful before 1935.

Seniority became a matter of public interest after unions became powerful. Since seniority is a right contractually conceived—it is not provided for in legislation–powerful unions and a sympathetic legal structure were essential to push the seniority clause. Traditional economic theory did not support job protection, and unions pushing for seniority filled a need.

The employer agreeing to a seniority provision does so reluctantly. Some employers endorse the use of seniority to reduce labor turnover, improve morale in the plant, reduce grievances, etc.; employers readily accept seniority to determine layoff, recall, and choice of shift. But employers reluctantly approve of seniority for promotion and training for better jobs. Where employees are paid on a piece-rate basis or production is closely regulated, the employer has less need to object to a seniority clause than where employees are paid on an hourly basis or where production cannot be predetermined. Employers seek to modify the straight seniority clause by also turning to skill, ability, reliability, and even family status for purposes of promotion. Furthermore, it is sometimes diplomatically unwise for the employer to resist a system which rewards the loyal employee. Union members, at least older union members, favor seniority clauses because the loyal employee is rewarded for past services, the older employee operating less efficiently is protected, company favoritism and antiunion animus is eliminated, etc.

Union leaders push for the wide-reaching seniority clause because:

1. It constitutes positive evidence of union value; old members are protected and new members are attracted.
2. Older members are protected from layoff or discharge, members who find it difficult to secure other employment.
3. Older members are more influential in the union than younger members.

Seniority can cause internal dissension and lead to political headaches for the union leader.[344] Younger members often feel that the union-initiated seniority clause is discriminatory, a feeling that disappears with age. Racial discrimination was often evident in the seniority clause negotiated prior to 1964 even though the possibility existed of a federal violation.[345] The Civil Rights Act specifically outlaws a seniority system which is not "bona fide,"[346] and the overt racially discriminatory contractual clause has disappeared. Nevertheless, employers and unions cling to tradition and camouflage the discriminatory seniority system.

The seniority clause and legislative push for fair employment sometimes clash head-on. Job equality must be expedited, and seniority discriminatorily accumulated in the past retards black advancement. Where past injustice is uncorrected, the black community fears the continuation of white discrimination. To the person facing discrimination, pointing to the constitutional, economic, and social difficulties of correcting past discrimination is useless. Employers, unions, and white employees are dead set against tampering with past seniority, while some blacks object to change injurious to them.[347] Seniority today is a sensitive issue and the judiciary reaches a fair solution with obvious strain.[348]

Bargaining patterns in industry were influenced by the Railway Labor Act of 1926,[349] the Wagner Act of 1935,[350] and the Taft-Hartley Act of 1947,[351] before fair employment was made a specific legislative goal. Prior to the Civil Rights Act of 1964, courts looked at the fairness of collective bargaining contracts to protect the black.[352] (Some seniority systems could have been protested under state fair employment laws.) The courts developed the notion that the Railway Labor Act and Taft-Hartley Act demand that the union must bargain for and represent the black in a fair manner.

Few blacks challenged the developing discriminatory patterns in seniority even though legal channels were open to check abuse. Lacking funds, distrusting white justice, or lacking information, blacks failed to protest the build-up of white seniority, a failure that will be difficult to rectify today.

Because of legislative will[353] and the constitutional difficulty of hitting at what has occurred in the past, limiting the reach of past seniority gathered in a discriminatory manner is difficult. If seniority did not serve any useful purpose, legislation could be considered outlawing its use. Seniority, however, like testing and the hiring hall, serves some useful purpose, and total condemnation is undesirable.

The employer is receptive to suggestions to overhaul the seniority system, not because of the black but a desire to do away with straight seniority for promotion. Some employers holding government contracts have been forced to consider changes in seniority provisions to avoid a charge of discrimination.[354]

The seniority clause can be based on length of service in a job, department, plant, or company, a series of interrelated jobs woven into a line of progression, age, etc.[355] Now that hiring, retention, and promotion must follow the rules calling for fair employment, the seniority provision must be negotiated with greater care than before to protect the white member and to avoid a charge of discrimination.

Seniority provisions openly discriminatory are easily detected and dealt with. For example, separate seniority lists for black and white are outlawed by Title VII. Clauses openly discriminatory are no longer negotiated and it is now important to look closely at the effect of the agreement upon the black. Even this is not always helpful because divisions are made, which are sometimes unfair, without violating Title VII.

Title VII is violated where one line of progression is reserved for the white employee and another for the black employee even though both lines are essentially equal in pay and opportunity. Where the seniority system is not geared to black or white jobs, the court must look at the type of work performed, opportunity for promotion, and pay scale to determine whether the arrangement is discriminatory.

Some black employees are unwilling to move into an integrated line of progression to avoid losing the accumulation of seniority. To move into a more desirable line of progression can mean the loss of seniority and pay, forcing the black to start at the bottom. Starting at the bottom may be necessary due to skill differentials, but it spells white racism to the black forced to give up past seniority and suffer a loss of earnings. The white currently in a favorable line of progression is protected by law even where there was past discrimination, while the black clawing his way upward is told that he cannot claim past seniority in order to progress currently.

Many state fair employment laws do not mention seniority specifically; it would appear that a state commission or court would have greater freedom to rule that seniority accumulated in the past on a discriminatory basis is illegal if it has a current impact. In spite of the protection extended by Congress to the accumulation of seniority, it is still possible to get around Section 703 (h) where the black is currently injured. For example, there may be a "pattern" of discrimination, permitting the Attorney General to intercede under Section 707.

Where discrimination has been practiced, a plant or company-wide system of seniority boosts somewhat the long-time black worker, while separate lines of progression, job, and departmental seniority favor the white worker. If this analysis is correct, contracts calling for seniority on the basis of job, department, or line of progression are preferred by the discriminating union.[356] Where seniority is plant or company-wide, the union seeking change desires to promote the interests of white members.

Section 703 (h) permits "different standards of compensation, or different terms, conditions, or privileges of employment pursuant to a bona fide seniority . . . system. . . ." The employer negotiating a "bona fide" agreement is protected by Section 703. While Section 703 (h) mentions the employer only, the union, and not the employer, pushes for a seniority clause. If the agreement is not "bona fide," both the employer and union are responsible under Section 703 (a) and (c).

The Taft-Hartley Act requires the employer and union to bargain in good faith over wages, hours, and working conditions.[357] Seniority is tied to wages, hours, and working conditions and, hence, constitutes a bargainable subject. Seniority leads to promotion, which determines wages and working conditions. Seniority affects layoff and recall, which are directly linked to wages and hours. An employer can refuse to negotiate with a union if the subject matter is considered discretionary, but bargaining is mandatory where the subject matter is closely tied to wages, hours, and working conditions. Consequently, seniority is a mandatory bargaining subject.[358] However, the racially discriminatory seniority clause does violate the good faith bargaining requirements of the Taft-Hartley Act.[359] A position can be taken that federal law promotes the inclusion of a seniority clause in a collective bargaining agreement. If the employer must bargain over seniority, some type of clause is inevitable; most collective bargaining agreements contain some type of seniority clause.

The only guidance provided by Congress in Title VII is the "bona fide" seniority system mentioned in Section 703 (h). Senator Clark said:

> First, it has been asserted that Title VII would undermine vested rights of seniority. . . . Title VII would have no effect on seniority rights existing at the time it takes effect. If, for example, a collective bargaining contract provides that in the event of layoffs, those who were hired last must be laid off first, such a provision would not be affected in the least by Title VII. This would be true even . . . where . . . white workers had more seniority than Negroes. . . . Of course, if the seniority rule itself is discriminatory, it would be unlawful. . . . But, in the ordinary case, assuming that seniority rights were built up over a period of time during which Negroes were not hired (or kept separate), these rights would not be set aside by . . . Title VII.[360]

Section 703 (a)(2) outlaws efforts to "limit, segregate, or classify . . . in any way which would deprive or tend to deprive any individual of employment opportunities or otherwise adversely affect his status as an employee. . . ." A seniority system may not be "bona fide" if an employee is limited, segregated, or classified in an adverse manner. A seniority system could "deprive any individual of employment opportunities" so that the court must look beyond the "individual" to determine what is "bona fide." The impact upon the class of employees is important rather than the impact upon the "individual" in the final analysis. Section 703 (a)(2) protects employees only while Section 703 (a) (1) prohibits discrimination in "compensation, terms, conditions, or privileges of employment," protecting "any individual" job applicant and employee.

Distinctions in "compensation, terms, conditions, or privileges of employment" are inevitable, and seniority systems "limit, segregate, or classify," injuring individual members of majority and minority groups. Racial and religious discrimination must be intentional, outwardly manifested at the group, to constitute wrongdoing under Title VII. Where the seniority provision is fair, differences in treatment or terms between black and white may not constitute intentional wrongdoing. More specifically, it is impossible to devise a seniority system which treats each individual equally, and some distinction between groups is unavoidable.

Section 703 (c)(2) restricts the union in a manner similar to the employer, outlawing discriminatory job referrals and discrimination on the job. The union is forbidden "to limit, segregate, or classify . . . in any way which would . . . tend to deprive any individual of employment opportunities, or would limit such employment opportunities. . . ." In addition, where seniority determines eligibility for apprentice training, "or other training or retraining," Section 703 (d) prohibits employer and union discrimination.

Several avenues are open to the courts to resolve seniority disputes.[361] One solution is to leave untouched the past accumulation of seniority in a discriminatory manner, providing the current clause in the collective bargaining agreement is nondiscriminatory. This solution has been applied in the railroad industry,[362] an approach that damages least seniority patterns established in the past without disturbing too much the immediate future. The strict constructionist will find this the most inviting alternative, an approach that retards or slows the quest for fair employment.

The ideal approach, from the black point of view, is to end the white stranglehold on the job market and minimize the discriminatory impact of seniority. Thus, if seniority has been accumulated in the past on a discriminatory basis, it should not be permitted to count currently. If a discriminatory seniority system of the past has promoted a white employee, the black would have a right to bump him. Consequently, the white forced to give up a job acquired before July 2, 1965, the date that the Civil Rights Act went into effect, would be punished retroactively, contrary to congressional will. This approach also presents serious constitutional hurdles.

A middle-of-the-road solution may be acceptable to the jurist. The black in the plant accumulating the necessary seniority, but not in the right job, could bid for an unfilled but more desirable job, as though his seniority entitled him to promotion. In effect, this suggestion means that a system of plant-wide seniority would be used. This approach may be legally acceptable because it would only apply to jobs currently vacant—the court looks to the present and not the past—while the past discriminatory seniority system is not permitted to hinder black promotion. The black bidding for a job could complain to the EEOC within ninety days after upgrading is refused.

Employers and white employees would resist, claiming economic injury because the black is not properly skilled and the system of plant-wide seniority would be tantamount to reverse discrimination. Concerning the claim of reverse discrimination, limiting the effect of past discrimination that has a current impact seems reasonable. In fact, a failure to minimize the effect of past discrimination is a far more heinous crime than failing to extend a helping hand, currently, to the black. Where the skills required in the current job and the one sought are similar or picked up rapidly, objection to black promotion seems ill-advised. But where jobs are dissimilar or the job sought requires great skill slowly developed, solution is more difficult. The following options are open to the court: the black could be paid the equivalent of the better position while remaining on the same job; the employer could foot the bill to prepare the black for the better job; the employer and union could jointly bear the cost of preparing the black for transfer to a better job; or a decision could be made that the employer cannot be punished for past discrimination. Government "seed money" may be necessary if the employer is forced to push a black into a job that he is not qualified to handle.

Discussion to this point has centered about the black employee with seniority who has not progressed because of discrimination. The newly hired black cannot point to the discriminatory seniority system of the past since it could not have hampered him. The only question that a court will face when the newly hired black tests the seniority system is whether it is currently discriminatory.

Where standards for promotion and job-bidding have been changed by a recent collective bargaining agreement, whether the seniority system is "bona fide" requires careful consideration. Unions only reluctantly agree to promotion on the basis of ability, although a substantial number of agreements follow the "heads and shoulders" principle in addition to straight seniority. Courts should carefully weigh a seniority system that, for the first time, emphasizes ability as a factor in promotion. Resorting to an ability or personality test for promotion may be a sign of bad faith. Recently requiring a high school diploma for promotion in addition to seniority is suspicious.

Two cases involving the same firm illustrate the difficulty of keeping within the confines of Title VII.[363] Prior to 1964, the employer and the union maintaining separate locals agreed to separate lines of promotion for black and white. The Civil Rights Act outlawed the segregated local, a per se violation,[364] as well as the discriminatory system of seniority. After the locals were integrated and the discriminatory seniority system abolished, the federal government, per Executive Order 11246, threatened to cancel a contract let to the employer because of discrimination against the black employee. The court took the position that Title VII is violated when past discrimination affects the current seniority status.

Arguing that a seniority system is collectively negotiated by employer and union, the union objected to the court remedy providing for plant-wide seniority. The court reasoned it was authorized by Congress to fashion a suitable remedy, at least until the employer and union are able to come up with a better suggestion. What is important is that the court approved a system of plant-wide seniority in order to minimize the impact of past discrimination.

CHAPTER NINE ❧ PROCEDURAL PROBLEMS

Filing Charges

Section 706 (a) of Title VII provides for the submission of a written complaint under oath to the EEOC before suit can be brought in a federal district court. A request for information from the EEOC and a state commission is not the equivalent of a complaint—Section 706 (a) requires a formal complaint.[365] A member of the commission can make a written complaint to the EEOC, but apparently an oath is not required.

Section 706 (d) requires the complaint to "be filed within ninety days after the alleged unlawful employment practice. . . .", a rule binding on the aggrieved party and the EEOC member preferring a charge. A written complaint made to the EEOC within the ninety-day period but later attested is timely.[366] However, the ninety-day time limitation does not apply to a charge made by the Attorney General finding a "pattern" of discrimination prohibited by Section 707. There are practical reasons for accepting initially the unattested charge: the typical complainant is unfamiliar with technicality, and the merit of the charge, not technicality, is important.

Section 706 (e) allots "thirty days" for EEOC conciliation, which can "be extended to not more than sixty days" after the complaint is made. The time limit set in Section 706 (e) does not appear to permit deviation—an amicable agreement between the EEOC and an employer must be reached in not "more than sixty days." That Congress permitted an extension "to not more than sixty days" indicates a desire to avoid additional delay. If the thirty- and sixty-day time limitation was intended to force the EEOC to expedite the handling of complaints, congressional will is understandable. However, if Section 706 (e) is a mandatory provision, justice can be subverted for no apparent reason. Because the EEOC has not been able to meet the sixty-day deadline, considerable attention has been given to Section 706 (e) by the courts. Concern was voiced that insufficient time had been allotted by Congress for EEOC conciliation when the Civil Rights Act was considered. The EEOC has averaged eleven months to investigate a complaint and an additional five months to conciliate.[367] It can be assumed that the average time taken by the EEOC to investigate and conciliate will be reduced in the future, but it is doubtful whether the sixty-day limitation is practical.

Another hangup in Section 706 (e) is that suit must be brought within thirty days after the expiration of the sixty-day period of conciliation; should the effort fail to obtain "voluntary compliance . . . the Commission shall so notify the person aggrieved and a civil action may, within thirty days (after the sixty-day period provided for conciliation) . . . be brought. . . ." While an adequate explanation can be presented when the EEOC does not meet the sixty-day deadline, the complainant will have difficulty explaining a delay of more than thirty days after hearing from the EEOC. With the EEOC averaging sixteen months to investigate and conciliate, the congressional timetable of filing suit within ninety days cannot be met.

The courts have taken an equitable approach rather than follow the time designated to Section 706 (e). The equitable approach is sound since Congress, evidently, did not believe the probability that more than sixty days would be required to investigate and conciliate. The grievant has been permitted to bring suit in a federal district court within thirty days after notification even though the EEOC exceeds the sixty-day statutory period allotted for conciliation.[368] One court felt that the sixty-day time limitation hung on the EEOC is directive and not mandatory.[369] The rationale advanced to support the directive interpretation was that conciliation benefits the complainant, and the public quest for fair employment should not be hindered because the EEOC cannot meet a deadline. Apparently, suing within thirty days after actual notification by the EEOC was interpreted as a mandatory provision. The thirty-day time period can be stretched where informal notice is given by the EEOC to the complainant that the attempt at conciliation was unsuccessful—time tolls only after formal notice.[370]

While we can agree with the decision allowing suit within thirty days after the complainant is notified irrespective of the length of time taken by the EEOC to conciliate, the court's labeling of Section 706 (e) as directional leads to difficulty. If the sixty-day conciliation period is directive, there is nothing to support the position that the thirty days allotted to bring suit is mandatory. Furthermore, if the sixty-day period is directional only, presumably an injured party would have the right to petition for court relief *before* the time expires. Permitting the grievant to sue after the sixty-day period expires but within thirty days after notification is the correct position; justice demands such an approach since the complainant is not at fault. But the logic supporting this position—the directive character of the legislation—could lead, as indicated, to problems.

One federal district court decided that a suit is proper after the EEOC rules, without undertaking conciliation, that the evidence does not substantiate the charge.[371] Conciliation is not undertaken unless the EEOC finds some evidence of racial discrimination. This decision is difficult to square with Section 706 (e) which permits suit "within thirty days" after "the Commission has been unable to obtain voluntary compliance. . . ." Furthermore, Section 706 (a) authorizes the Commission to seek "voluntary compliance" when "there is reasonable cause to believe that the charge is true. . . ." To assure fair play and avoid constitutional difficulty, assuming that Congress did not intend to bar court relief when the EEOC does not uncover evidence of wrongdoing is the best approach.

The same issue raises another question. The EEOC cannot publicize a dispute under consideration.[372] If the Commission cannot publicize a dispute, can the EEOC member disagreeing with the majority decision that the evidence does not support the charge sue in a federal district court because of the publicity? Since the prohibition only applies to the EEOC, the ban on publicity would not prevent an injured party from pressing his point of view. Leaders of minority organizations, aware that widespread publicity is often more meaningful than conciliation, can go to court to take advantage of the possible publicity.

Whether the plaintiff can sue before the EEOC undertakes conciliation is a question that has been raised. Presumably the plaintiff must wait out the statutory sixty-day period allotted for investigation and conciliation; the propriety of going to court before the EEOC undertakes conciliation arises only after sixty days elapse. One court of appeals approved of a court suit without the EEOC attempting conciliation.[373] Another court, reaching a somewhat different solution, felt that a court suit is proper so long as *some* effort to conciliate, even though incomplete, was made by the EEOC.[374] But some effort to conciliate would have to be made by the EEOC before the court could extend the welcome sign. Other courts take the position that the EEOC effort to reach an amicable solution must be finished before court suit is authorized by Section 706 (g).[375] Plaintiffs and the EEOC (as an intervening party) have claimed that conciliation can be bypassed because of the backlog of complaints awaiting the EEOC, pointing to Section 706 (a)—"the Commission shall endeavor to eliminate any . . . alleged unlawful employment practice by informal methods of conference, conciliation and persuasion. . . ." They contend that Section 706 (a) does not require EEOC intervention before court suit can be brought. Because congressional intent was not expressed in Section 706 (a), the exhaustion of EEOC effort could be implied if voluntary and conciliatory methods are best suited to end discrimination in employment.

Section 706 (a), as indicated, permits suit by a member of the EEOC where there is "reasonable cause to believe a violation. . . ." This raises the question of whether an EEOC member electing to bring suit must follow the time limitations and sue within ninety days after the complaint is made. Since the EEOC member can determine if the deadline can be met, it can be reasoned that the ninety-day period must be followed. In contrast, an injured party may be unaware of the time limitation and progress made by the EEOC.

Section 706 (b) does not mention that the complainant must turn to the EEOC before bringing a civil suit, while Section 706 (a) makes mandatory a written charge under oath to the EEOC. Inconclusive evidence points to a Congressional intent to permit the plaintiff to bypass the EEOC.[376] But Sections 706 (a) and (b) can be read together so that EEOC conciliation is necessary before turning to the court. Since courtroom technique is ill-suited to deal with employment discrimination, giving the EEOC first crack at solving the problem seems logical. Furthermore, Title VII was to a large extent modeled after state law which requires that a commission resolve the dispute before turning to a court. Yet the rationale used calling for prior adjudication by a state commission does not fully apply to the EEOC because it is without authority to make a decision.

As could be anticipated, courts would face this jurisdictional question. There is unanimous agreement that a complaint must be made to the EEOC before suit is brought under Section 706 (f).[377] Even where a state commission dismisses a complaint referred to it by the EEOC for lack of probable cause, the federal commission must investigate and conciliate before suit is brought in a federal district court.[378]

While a complaint to the EEOC is a prerequisite to bringing a suit, an injured party can seek an injunction to stop employer malpractices without turning to the EEOC.[379] But Title VII does not specifically authorize a request for an injunction by a private party. The Attorney General has access to the federal courts without petitioning the EEOC. The Attorney General who "has reasonable cause to believe that" there is "a pattern or practice of resistance" can request an injunction or other relief before the merit of the charge is weighed.[380] Since Section 707 (a) authorizes the Attorney General to request injunctive aid, the Norris-La Guardia Act, which limits the use of the injunction against unions involved in a labor dispute, was amended where unions discriminate. Furthermore, since the Attorney General requests the injunction, it can be reasoned that the Norris-La Guardia does not control since it was aimed at stopping employer-secured injunctions.[381] Should an injured party seek an injunction against a union, the Norris-La Guardia Act was amended by Section 706 (g), permitting the court to "enjoin the respondent from engaging in such unlawful employment practice. . . ."

State Commissions

Congress took more than twenty years to pass fair employment legislation, permitting many states to develop a comprehensive regulatory system. Concerned with the preservation of state rights and full use of past experience, Congress considering federal legislation favored state jurisdiction in several ways. Section 708 emphatically provides that "(n)othing in this title shall . . . exempt or relieve any person from any liability, duty, penalty, or punishment provided by any present or future law of any state. . . ." Section 708 protects state jurisdiction to the point where penalties can be imposed under state or federal law.

Section 709 encourages cooperation between the EEOC and state agencies, permitting the former to "utilize the services of . . . (state) agencies" and to "reimburse such agencies . . . for services rendered. . . ." Section 709 (b) also provides that the EEOC and state commissions "may enter into written agreements" by which the EEOC "shall refrain from processing a charge . . . and under which no person may bring a civil action under Section 706. . . ."[382] To date, federal jurisdiction has not been relinquished to a state commission.

Section 706 (b) assigns priority of jurisdiction to the state with a fair employment law even though an agreement is not reached with the EEOC. If the state or local law, whether civil or criminal, prohibits discrimination in employment, Section 706 (b) forbids the EEOC to process a complaint "before the expiration of sixty days after proceedings have been commenced under the State or local law, unless . . . earlier terminated. . . ." Where an EEOC member prefers a charge, Section 706 (c) calls for a moratorium of at least sixty days to allow state adjustment (additional time can be agreed to). The Attorney General charging "a pattern or practice of resistance" can "bring a civil action in the appropriate district court" without waiting for state adjudication. In summation, state priority is called for in Title VII where the complainant is an employee, prospective employee, or member of the EEOC; on the other hand, the Attorney General can file suit under Section 707 without waiting for state consideration.

Section 706 (b) does not define a "proceeding" under "State or local law" and does not require a state administrative-type statute; state priority of jurisdiction is preserved when there is "a State or local law prohibiting the unlawful employment practice and establishing or authorizing a State or local authority to grant or seek relief from such practice or to institute criminal proceedings thereto. . . ." The typical state law springing up since World War II to control discrimination uses administrative technique, with civil action to follow if necessary; the federal law protects state jurisdiction where a criminal statute controls. Since criminal prosecution has not been successful in the past, Section 706 (b) should be amended to end priority of state regulation. To date, the courts have followed a straight line: where *substantial* relief is available under state law (neither Section 706 (b) nor (c) mentions "substantial" relief, only the need for a state law), the in-

110

jured party or EEOC member must pursue the remedy provided by state law before seeking federal aid.[383]

The Availability of Other Remedies

A recurring question is the availability of a remedy, other than a state fair employment law, and the impact on the initial jurisdiction of the EEOC. A member of the EEOC or the Attorney General claiming a "pattern" of discrimination can proceed under Title VII irrespective of the availability of alternative remedies. But a question of an election of remedy is raised where the injured party can seek relief elsewhere. For example, can the claimant seek aid under a collective bargaining contract if an adequate remedy is available, bypassing Title VII? Can an aggrieved party turn to another administrative agency, such as the NLRB, before petitioning the EEOC? A supplemental question is whether an award by an arbitrator or other administrative agency binds the court in a Title VII suit.

The courts take the position that relief under Title VII is proper even though aid may be available under a collective bargaining agreement or through the National Railway Adjustment Board.[384] In the railroad industry, the black hoping to turn to arbitration or to the National Railway Adjustment Board, controlled by employer and union, wastes his time and effort. Consequently, direct court relief has been permitted. Where the NLRB functions, a remedy may be available, possibly superior to that provided by the EEOC. Title VII provides for EEOC investigation and conciliation and subsequent court involvement if suit is brought by an injured party, a member of the EEOC, or the Attorney General, and Congress showed no interest in forcing the use of another remedy. Since the principal thrust of another remedy, like the collective bargaining contract and other legislation, is something other than discrimination in employment, limiting the claimant's choice appears to be unwise. Moreover, the Supreme Court has already endorsed plaintiff choice of remedy via the administrative or court route.[385]

Arbitrators sometimes deal with employment discrimination after an administrative agency denies the petition for relief. An arbitrator sometimes tackles discrimination because the collective bargaining agreement calls for a decision in spite of the jurisdiction of a state commission or the EEOC.[386] In the absence of total satisfaction for the petitioner and the dissimilarity of proceeding under a state law, some arbitrators feel compelled to make an award, ignoring legislative and judicial remedies. The validity of this rationale increases where a state criminal statute controls or where a state commission must follow legal rules of evidence, such as in Kansas, Oklahoma, Utah,[387] and Illinois;[388] the evidence acceptable and the remedy au-

111

thorized legislatively may be more restrictive than when the arbitrator plays his hand. This rationale is also convincing where the EEOC plays a role—it can only conciliate. But where a state commission attempts conciliation and later makes a binding decision, the arbitartor's rationale favoring the coexistence of a legal and contractual remedy is less convincing unless the remedy proves inadequate. State commissions not required to follow the hearsay rules of evidence function similarly to an arbitrator. There is, however, substantial difference in the event of appeal; an arbitrator's decision is not reviewable,[389] while the decision of a state commission is subject to judicial scrutiny.

A federal district court decided that a ruling by an arbitrator and state fair employment commission does not bar a complaint under Title VII.[390] The court reasoned that the election of remedy defense presented by the employer was not convincing because the arbitrator was limited by the language of the collective bargaining agreement and the grievant was not represented by legal counsel. As indicated in the previous paragraph, another difference is that the court cannot question the facts or the legal position relied upon by the arbitrator. On the other hand, a court suit can be brought, and appeal can be taken under the Civil Rights Act.

There is another school of thought: when the plaintiff seeks aid under a collective bargaining contract, a remedy is selected, barring help under state or federal legislation.[391] This approach not only limits the public quest for fair employment but the person claiming discrimination may be unaware of his alternatives. The election of remedy bar conflict will have to be settled by a higher court.

The NLRB, because of Section 10 (a) of the Taft-Hartley Act,[392] is not required to relinquish jurisdiction to an arbitrator. But the NLRB honors an arbitration award dealing with an unfair labor practice if the proceeding is procedurally fair, the decision is binding, and public policy declared in the Taft-Hartley Act is not thwarted.[393] It is not necessary to adopt such an approach at the present time under Title VII because the EEOC can only conciliate. Even if the EEOC decision is followed in court, there is something to be said for permitting a complainant to explore many avenues of relief until satisfactorily resolved. Where relief is denied because of a procedural limitation, like the admissibility of evidence or a statute of limitation, other avenues should remain open.

Funding

There are thirty-three states with commissions administering laws which outlaw discrimination in employment for racial or religious reasons. Four additional states outlaw such discrimination by criminal statute. The remaining thirteen states do not outlaw racial discrimination in employment, but three of them prohibit discrimination due to age.[394] While the administrative-type statute is generally conceded to be the most effective, there is no assurance these laws are adequately enforced. The enforcement agencies may be understaffed or underfinanced, or the citizenry may be unaware of the services of the commission.

The adequacy of funds is difficult to determine, but several methods can be turned to to measure adequacy. One technique is to compare per capita or per black spending on enforcing fair employment laws among the states. Another method is to look at the activities of the commissions to get some indication of their effectiveness.

Data on the appropriations for, and some of the activities of, the commissions have been received by the authors from 23 states.[395] This information is summarized in Table 1.

The total amount appropriated to the twenty-three state commissions has increased substantially in recent years—from $6.2 million in 1966 to $10 million in 1968, but not all of these funds are for use to enforce fair employment laws. In sixteen states, the commission administers a fair housing law as well as a fair employment law. Total expenditures or appropriations in the twenty-three states range from $2,500 to $2,980,281 in 1968. On a per capita basis, they range from less than one cent in New Hampshire to twenty-eight cents in Alaska. On the basis of cost per black, the range was from thirteen cents in Illinois to $14.13 in Hawaii. Since these commissions are also responsible for enforcing the law with respect to age or sex discrimination in all but four of these states, those with relatively few blacks should spend substantially more per black. Yet, the relationship is not very close. Although there is a wide range in expenditure, we find sixteen of the states ranging from forty-two cents to $2.64 per black. Within this range, there is little relationship between the percentage of black population and expenditure per black.

We expected to find that those states with a high percentage of blacks would have a relatively high per capita expenditure per annum on fair employment enforcement. This expectation is not substantiated by the data. There is no discernible relationship between the proportion of a state's black population and per capita expenditures to enforce housing and employment discrimination laws. For example, the median per capita expenditure in the nine states in which blacks account for 5 per cent or more of the population is six cents; it is also six cents per capita in the fourteen states where blacks account for less than 5 per cent of the population.

The great variance in per capita and per black expenditure suggests that inadequate funds are appropriated in many states. It is unlikely that state commissions have more money than is needed. Accordingly, those states which rank low in per capita expenditure probably appropriate an

113

Table 1
State FEPC Appropriations and Activities

State	Population[a] (in thousands)		Appropriation[b] (thousands of dollars)				Complaints Handled			
	Total[a]	Negro	1965	1966	1967	1968	1965	1966	1967	1968
Alaska	265	7	38.6	49.7	55.5	74.9	22	20	40	107
Ariz.	1,603	43	35.0	32.2	36.4	39.5	c	16	37	40
Calif.	18,802	884	710.0	800.0	825.0	849.0	887	817	1,112	1,523
Colo.	1,955	40	114.2	124.3	156.9	205.0	132	227	224	411
Conn.	2,878	107	181.3	183.5	312.8	443.4	138	209	219	252
Hawaii	727	5	0	.3	.4	11.3	5	9	9	13
Ill.	10,786	1,037	97.5	97.5	137.5	137.5	201	325	769	1,032
Ind.	4,951	269	65.0	65.0	114.0	114.0	158	163	215	210
Kansas	2,275	91	60.6	63.2	84.1	132.8	35	61	47	103
Ky.	3,181	216	45.9	156.8	179.2	202.1	0	16	54	43
Mich.	8,468	718	634.4	943.7	1,391.6	1,893.4	423	787	1,106	c
Minn.	3,572	22	81.3	79.4	163.3	175.3	176	251	92	293
Mo.	4,564	391	164.8	217.7	296.5	352.9	97	433	246	297
Neb.	1,439	29	26.3	26.3	51.0	51.0	2	17	43	56
N.H.	676	2	c	0	2.5	2.5	c	4	0	2
N.J.	6,899	515	c	c	341.0	537.0	c	627	673	775
N.Y.	18,205	1,418	c	2,104.3	2,718.4	2,980.3	1,315	1,360	1,588	2,175
Ohio	10,364	786	205.0	248.4	242.6	423.1	164	550	425	611
Oregon	1,973	18	c	59.7	77.3	94.8	c	85	81	99
Pa.	11,601	853	655.9	693.7	835.9	878.6	444	480	360	632
R.I.	898	18	47.5	50.9	67.5	74.2	47	36	43	c
W.Va.	1,809	89	c	51.0	78.9	102.4	c	c	50	37
Wis.	4,167	75	102.9	107.1	134.0	191.0	60	79	86	118

a Source: *Statistical Abstract of the United States,* 1968, pp. 12, 27; total population figures are 1966 estimates; Negro population data are for 1960.

b Fiscal years in some cases. Some arbitrary allocation of biennial appropriations has been made. These data secured from questionnaires submitted by the state agencies.

c No data submitted.

inadequate sum to enforce fair employment laws. It is doubtful, of course, that even those with relatively high expenditures have adequately funded their state commission.

The information available indicates that many states have inadequate facilities and staffs. In some states, commission members are paid while in some they are not; in some states, they only receive expenses. Some states use directors, some do not. Directors' salaries in 1968 varied from $31,660 to $10,000. Most states listed no expenditures for trial and hearing examiners, but in each of two states such expenditures exceeded half a million dollars in 1968.

The number of branch offices operated gives some indication of the reach of the commission. In six states with few blacks, the commission had no branch offices, while Michigan listed ten and New York fourteen. The remainder had from one to four branch offices.[396]

The number of complaints alleging discrimination in housing or employment increased in almost every state from 1965 to 1968. The increase undoubtedly reflects greater awareness of the law, increased activities of the agencies, and a bit more trust in white-dominated justice. Again there is great variance among states. Much of this variance can be explained by the number of blacks in the states and the expenditures made by the state commissions.

The total number of complaints received in the twenty-three states in 1968 was 10,041—7,625 concerning employment and 2,416 housing. There were eight states in which less than 100 complaints were received in 1968, eight in which the number was between 100 and 500, three in which the number was between 500 and 1,000, and three with more than 1,000.[397] New York, with 2,175, had the largest number of complaints. The number of complaints received in each state still seems rather small, but it is difficult to evaluate this factor. Moreover, we must remember that the laws probably have some deterrent effect so these numbers understate the impact.

It should be remembered that this discussion has been limited to state fair employment commissions. The federal FEPC is also active in these states, so the above figures understate the amount of activity underway to to enforce fair employment practices.

CHAPTER TEN ✂ MANPOWER PROGRAMS

A number of programs designed to improve the quality of human capital are currently funded by the federal government. Those which involve education or training are frequently referred to as manpower programs.

Manpower programs include schooling and formal classroom training of some type, on-the-job training with private industry, and specialized programs servicing specific groups of people with particular needs. Classroom and on-the-job training are available to the general population, but a higher percentage of blacks than whites are assisted by these programs. The third category of programs, designed for specific groups, frequently helps minority groups, especially blacks.

Schools in this country can help the manpower development programs in three ways. The first and most obvious is to provide the best possible education for people of school age. The second is to provide remedial education and training for those without adequate preparation. The third function is to provide continuing education to update the skills of those who need and desire such training.

Federal aid to elementary and secondary school education currently totals about 3.3 billion dollars annually.[398] The bulk of this money is to upgrade the quality of general education in schools in low-income areas or areas in which a high percentage of the population is employed by the federal government. In actual practice, federal funds are siphoned off to relatively prosperous school districts. There are no data available to show how much of this aid does go to the poor and to the black. But it is clear that most of it is aimed at those whose parents are on the low end of income distribution. In 1968, $1.8 billion of these funds went to assistance for educationally deprived children or economic opportunity programs.[399] Presumably, a substantial number of those benefiting were black.

In addition to general aid to education, programs established under the Vocational Education Act of 1963 and the Vocational Education Amendments of 1968 prepare young people more adequately for their working life by teaching the specific skills needed in today's economy. Enrollment in federally aided vocational education programs reached 8.2 million in 1968. Table 1 shows enrollment figures by type of program in 1964 and 1967.

Some progress has been made through these programs. The unemployment rate for individuals enrolled in them is lower than for others in the same age bracket who were not enrolled. In general, graduates of these programs make a better transition into the labor force than those with the same number of years of schooling but no vocational education.[400]

There have been, however, rather serious shortcomings in the training provided under the Vocational Education Act. The National Advisory Council on Vocational Education criticized the type of training given and also felt that those who needed vocational education most were not receiving it.[401] Much of the training was outdated; insufficient effort was made to match supply and demand, especially in agricultural training where the number of enrollees outstripped demand.

The Council concluded that much of the apparent increase in enrollment was illusory. It simply reflected the inclusion of persons who had been receiving some form of vocational training but who were not formerly counted as vocational students.[402]

The Council also criticized the lack of data which permit evaluation of the relative needs for the various types of training given. The available data showed little effort to develop programs in areas with critical manpower shortages, such as health occupations and technical programs.

The major criticism of vocational education is that it has not reached the people who need it most in terms of location, race, and educational achievement. The Council found that the programs did not adequately meet the needs of the metropolitan dweller, especially the culturally and economically disadvantaged residing in the slum and ghetto neighborhood. The rural white has disproportionately benefited from vocational education, while the share of the urban black has been disproportionately small. Unfortunately, data are unavailable to pinpoint whether those facing racial discrimination receive an adequate share of the federal bounty. The Council concluded, however, that vocational education opportunities are inadequate for out-of-school youth. High school dropouts and unemployed high school graduates have not been well served by these programs.[403]

Those with academic, social, and economic handicaps were given special attention in the 1963 Act, but the Council found that little was accomplished. Vocational education tends to serve students substantially below others in general capability. Unfortunately, the better high schools frequently attempt to upgrade their student bodies to enhance their prestige by eliminating the poorer students through more stringent requirements rather than giving them the special help they may require.

In some school systems, vocational education is the dumping ground for academic misfits. Elsewhere, where vocational education leaders have a strong voice in policy determination, misfits are rejected and placed in schools with general curricula. As a general rule, the academically able

Table 1

Enrollments in Federally Aided Vocational
Technical Education, by Field of Education,
Fiscal Years 1964 and 1967

| | Number (thousands) | | Per Cent Distribution | |
| | Fiscal Year | | Fiscal Year | |
Field of Education	1964	1967	1964	1967
Total	4,566	7,048	100.0	100.0
Agriculture	861	935	18.9	13.3
Distributive	364	481	7.3	6.8
Health	59	115	1.3	1.6
Home economics	2,022	2,187	44.3	31.0
Office		1,572		22.3
Technical	221	266	4.8	3.8
Trades and Industry	1,0d9	1,491	23.4	21.2

Source: *Manpower Report of President, 1969*, p. 82.

students have been eligible for vocational education, while the least able have been rejected. These able students are sought by employers for industrial training programs. The students left out are those with low motivation and poor preparation, two handicaps which vocational education can help overcome. Many students, especially black, come from homes with low or different verbal skills than is tested. Vocational education emphasizes doing and can motivate the student to learn the academic and industrial skills necessary to hold a job. Here, many students learn for the first time that reading, arithmetic, and report writing are useful in the real world.[404]

In large cities, a higher proportion of black than white youth enroll in vocational courses, while the opposite is true elsewhere. Some of the higher than proportionate black enrollments in vocational schools in large cities may be due to the "dumping ground" tendencies and inadequate educational and social backgrounds. The data are skimpy, but they suggest that blacks are underrepresented in vocational courses, postsecondary vocational education and adult extension courses in rural areas and small towns. Data from the Civil Rights Commission indicate that most vocational education is provided in segregated schools[405] offering training in lesser skills in black schools than in the predominantly white schools. Blacks tend to live in areas where all schools are in need of improvement.

Most of the Council's recommendations for improving vocational education were adopted in the Vocational Education Amendments of 1968.[406] The 1968 legislation stresses the expansion and improvement of vocational educational programs for those who need it most. Less emphasis is placed on traditional concepts and techniques and more is placed upon developing the maximum occupational potential of the physically and mentally handicapped and the socially and economically disadvantaged. Ten per cent of the basic vocational education grants to the states must be reserved for the physically and mentally handicapped. Fifteen per cent of the basic grants in fiscal 1970 and 25 per cent of future increases in these grants are to be used to aid those with academic, socioeconomic, or other handicaps, and additional funds are provided for special programs for the disadvantaged.[407] If successfully implemented, the path out of the ghetto and perpetual underemployment could become slightly less difficult.

The Manpower Development and Training Act

The Manpower Development and Training Act (MDTA) of 1962 provided for classroom or institutional training and on-the-job training (OJT). The program began in 1962 when the unemployment rate was relatively high (5.5 per cent), dictating the focus of the original MDTA programs. These projects were intended to provide training and rapid job placement for those who had been employed but were currently jobless. The majority of the trainees in the early projects were unemployed heads of households with at least three years of gainful employment. They were people considered capable of qualifying for employment within twelve months or less.

As the unemployment rate fell, the MDTA shifted emphasis to train the disadvantaged. The amount of resources devoted to this group has consistently risen. Trainees who are nonwhite have increased from 24 per cent in 1963 to 49 per cent in 1968.[408] The percentage with less than a high school education has gone from 41 to 60 per cent, and of those 21 years of age or less from 25 to 38 per cent in the same period. Some of this change is the natural consequence of a lower unemployment rate. In addition to the conscious change of program emphasis to help the black and the disadvantaged, few men and women who are unemployed today have the characteristics of the original MDTA trainees. However, the numbers trained are still small relative to the need. In 1968, there were 140,000 in institutional and 125,000 in OJT projects.[409]

The MDTA programs are less successful than they should be. There has been the inevitable problem of failing to teach skills for which there is a demand and a failing to reach people who need to be reached.[410] The following discussion makes it obvious that there has been a proliferation and dilution of programs under the MDTA (more than 120) which has reduced its effectiveness. Some should undoubtedly be phased out and others strengthened and expanded.

The MDTA was amended in 1963, 1965, 1966, and 1968 to correct weaknesses and meet the critical problems in manpower. The 1963 amendments, aimed at servicing groups with the highest incidence of unemployment,

119

changed the act in four major respects. One change was to provide more training for youths. The original purpose of the MDTA was to retrain older workers, but it was apparent that many young people were inadequately prepared to enter the labor market, especially members of minority groups. The second major change was to provide basic literacy education, in conjunction with occupational training, to equip the disadvantaged for employment.[411] Experience showed that many blacks required more than training in specific occupational skills; basic education was necessary to increase the effectiveness of training. Unfortunately, more basic education must be taught to maximize the benefits of job training. The third change was to increase allowances in order to provide enough income to permit the most disadvantaged trainees to undertake and complete their training. The fourth change was to relax eligibility requirements for training for both adults and youth. The original act specified that training be given to those who could reasonably expect employment, barring many disadvantaged workers. The relaxation of requirements brought more of the hard-core unemployed into the training programs.[412]

The 1965 amendments consolidated federal training programs by transferring the training provisions of the Area Redevelopment Act to the MDTA. Training allowances were further liberalized, extending the maximum period of payment, increasing the allotment for trainees with families, providing supplemental allowances for daily transportation costs, and further easing eligibility requirements.[413]

The 1966 amendments resulted in the initiation of orientation training to help develop good work habits and attitudes in trainees, and limited health services were authorized for MDTA enrollees. Because funds were not appropriated, little has been done to help those in poor health due to their economically disadvantageous background.[414]

Another MDTA amendment provided part-time training to qualify low-skill employees for better jobs. It was hoped that the upgrading of workers would help to meet shortages of skilled labor which, in turn, would open opportunities for disadvantaged persons at the bottom of the occupational ladder. Little headway has been made to date on this type of training.[415]

The developments discussed above contributed to the formal redirection of the program announced in 1966. It was then decided that 65 per cent of the entire MDTA training effort would be directed to reclaiming the hard-core unemployed. Special groups facing the greatest employment difficulties were identified and guidelines were established for their training. Blacks accounted for a disproportionate percentage of those placed in special group categories. The 65 per cent goal was reached in 1968; in fact, it reached 68 per cent.[416]

There were several MTDA amendments in 1968.[417] Most important, the disadvantaged and the black were given priority in the use of skill centers. At the outset, MDTA training projects were often set up, one at a time, in places where the need for training and the resources to train were available. When the trainees completed the course, sometimes the projects were repeated, sometimes they were terminated. As programs developed, single program operations became less common and multioccupational training centers more frequently serving the black community became dominant.

Fifty-five facilities providing occupational training for a number of skills plus the supportive services required by disadvantaged trainees were designated Manpower Training Skills Centers in 1968.[418] The growing recognition for supportive services made it important to provide basic education in conjunction with job training in the fifty-five facilities. As it has become increasingly obvious that adequate training for the disadvantaged cannot be accomplished without providing many services which were at first considered not to be "training," counselors were added to project staffs, arrangements were made with other agencies to supply medical and legal assistance, and other necessary services were supplied. The trend is in the direction of helping the disadvantaged by providing them with more and more supportive help. Due to inadequate funding, lack of direction, and fragmented effort, the fifty-five facilities are still not functioning up to snuff.

The MDTA launched the first major cooperative program between industry and government to alleviate critical manpower shortages by providing for on-the-job training to be conducted by employers on contract with the Department of Labor.[419] This program grew rapidly from 1963 to 1968, both for disadvantaged workers and those needing new skills to become employed. Enrollment has been reduced in 1969 as emphasis has been shifted to Job Opportunities in the Business Sector (JOBS) program but the total number of enrollees in on-the-job training programs (MDTA and JOBS) continues to increase.

Employers regarded OJT projects rather suspiciously in the initial years of the program, but that is changing. Given the success of many of these projects and the scarcity of skilled labor, many companies actively seek OJT projects; it is now recognized as a means of financing training to help workers and employers.

The training given through MDTA-OJT projects covers a wide variety of occupations. Most of the training has been for semiskilled labor, but some training has been provided for higher-level occupations such as draftsman and the licensed practical nurse. The OJT has trained the disadvantaged as well as provided skills needed by industry.

On-the-job training of a worker with an educational and cultural handicap has been helped through the use of "coupled projects." As with institutional training, it has become clear that the disadvantaged require more than training in specific occupational skills. The coupled projects combine skill training with basic education; training in communication skills and conventional or "acceptable" attitudes toward work are developed. More than one-third of all OJT enrollees in the fiscal year 1968 were in coupled projects.

Disadvantaged persons are difficult to recruit and retain, especially if much classroom training is involved or if a long time is spent in training. Those needing basic education are reluctant to stick with it. Their previous classroom experience was frequently limited to a crowded ghetto school which they could not stomach. Therefore, attempts to maintain trainee interest in coupled projects frequently involve education on the employer's premises rather than classes in schools.

There are many special programs within the MDTA-OJT programs, some of which are discussed below. This variety of projects presumably allows the OJT program to be "a versatile training vehicle that can be adapted to special objectives. . . ."[420] Unfortunately, it also means a multiplicity of projects hard to control and evaluate.

One type of OJT program is the Area Redevelopment Program to train workers for businesses in areas eligible for redevelopment assistance as designated by the Economic Development Administration. There are also MDTA institutional training programs in those areas. About 900 areas with a population of some 26 million, many of them black, have been declared eligible for redevelopment assistance. Unfortunately, the MDTA-OJT program has not reached many of those who need training.

During the fiscal year 1968, approximately 14,000 residents in redevelopment areas enrolled in OJT projects.[421] Most of the 14,000 were unemployed and many were members of minority groups. Many of these projects trained people in rural areas for local jobs. If the training is successful, people are kept from migrating to the cities and further adding to ghetto problems.

Another OJT program is the Labor Education Advancement Program (LEAP), or the outreach program, to foster apprentice training and train enrollees to pass apprentice entrance examinations. LEAP helps individuals find jobs as apprentices, usually in the construction trades. In late 1968, 1,700 minority youths were placed as apprentices in the building and construction trades by LEAP and another 800 training spots were authorized.[422] The number of black participants in apprentice programs registered with United States or state agencies doubled between spring, 1967, and the end of 1968.[423] Impressive as these statistics are, much remains to be done. There are 225,000 registered apprentices throughout the United

States, but fewer than 10,000 are blacks. Blacks held about 3.6 per cent of all apprenticeships in 1968, a disproportionately small number. However, this does represent significant progress over the 2.6 per cent figure in 1966.[424] Many companies, workers, and unions continue to oppose the use of black apprentices. In May, 1968, Undersecretary of Labor James J. Reynolds estimated that an acceptable number of apprenticeship appointments for blacks and other minorities would be reached within three years. The basis for his optimism was the growing number of apprentice outreach programs being conducted and supported by building and construction trades councils with the technical and financial assistance of the Department of Labor.

The OJT programs have been successful in terms of placement of the trainees. Of the 54,500 who completed OJT projects in 1967, 90 per cent were employed at the last post-training followup, mostly in training-related work. Employer and union reaction to MDTA-OJT training was generally favorable and continued cooperation is planned. Some feel that MDTA-OJT made it possible to train the disadvantaged and hard core, providing the necessary incentive for those whose qualifications were weak.[425] The major recommendations of the Department of Labor to improve OJT programs are more counseling, coaching, and other supportive services, more technical assistance to cooperating employers, and further streamlining of administration.

The MDTA institutional and OJT programs are worth the cost despite their shortcomings. The pilot benefit-cost studies of MDTA training programs indicate that they return more to society in one year than their cost to the federal government. The average net federal benefit-cost ratio, defined as the direct and indirect benefits to society (exclusive of increased taxes paid) compared to federal investment per trainee, is 3.28 to 1 for OJT and 1.10 to 1 for institutional training, a return realized only one year after training.[426] While there is no information on the lasting benefit, whether it will increase or decrease, the short-run desirability of the program is clear if these estimates are valid.

The institutional programs are considerably more expensive to the federal government than the OJT programs—$1,450 per trainee versus $650. In terms of benefit, measured by increased earnings, the institutional trainee has added to his earnings slightly more than the OJT trainee even though the OJT trainee typically receives a 30 to 50 per cent greater increase in hourly pay. The pay differential is as much due to the type of trainee involved as to the efficacy of the programs. Institutional trainees in the pilot study typically experienced longer periods of unemployment prior to training than on-the-job trainees. Therefore, the training programs reduced the average period of unemployment more than for those in the OJT programs. In the year after training, on-the-job trainees had a lower unemployment rate than did institutional trainees.

Job Opportunities in the Business Sector differ from the MDTA-OJT program in four important respects:

1) It (JOBS) serves only disadvantaged workers.
2) It only operates in the fifty largest urban areas.
3) It relies on employers to provide jobs, training, and the full range of supportive services required to help disadvantaged workers make a satisfactory job adjustment.
4) It utilizes the services and support of businessmen to help develop and promote the programs.

In the JOBS program, the employer hires the worker first and trains him afterward. There is considerable evidence that initial placement in a job at regular wages motivates a disadvantaged individual more than a training period coming before employment.[427]

The National Alliance of Businessmen (NAB) was formed to enlist the support of business for JOBS. A national executive board consisting of many top executives from major companies leads NAB. NAB undertook the responsibility of encouraging employers to pledge jobs for the program.

The cooperating companies provide jobs and training for hard-core unemployed workers, footing the normal cost of recruitment and training. The extra cost incurred to provide counseling, remedial education, prevocational training, etc., is offset by funds provided by the Department of Labor.

Special training is necessary for management personnel dealing with JOBS trainees. The typical trainee does not present the same disciplinary and behavior problems encountered from other employees. Accordingly, the Department of Labor and NAB sponsor a special sensitivity program to educate supervisory and management personnel as to the special needs and problems of the hard-core unemployed. A program to train rank-and-file workers as job coaches and counselors has also been developed in cooperation with the AFL-CIO. This program pairs sensitized workers and the hard-core unemployed to provide job adjustment assistance.

The JOBS goal is to place in industry half a million disadvantaged workers by June, 1971. In early 1969, the program was ahead of schedule, placing more than 100,000 workers.[428] The turnover rate among those hired averaged about 4 per cent per month, close to the normal rate of turnover for the positions involved.

As of November, 1968, 75 per cent of the JOBS employees were black, and 10 per cent carried Spanish surnames.[429] Their average level of education put them below the eleventh grade; unemployment averaged 23.7 weeks in the previous year; and average annual family income was $2,790.

It seems that the goal of training the disadvantaged is being followed in practice as well as in theory even though it is too early to assess the value of the JOBS program. However, it is accepted with considerably more enthusiasm by businessmen and the Nixon Administration than are other manpower programs. Part of this enthusiasm is undoubtedly due to a bias in favor of private over public enterprise. Many people feel that JOBS must be better than other programs be cause there is more business and less government involvement. Enthusiastic participation is an important element in the success of any program, so that biases, however rational or irrational, are important. Additionally, the JOBS program may well be better than previous programs, benefiting from past experience by permitting the trainee to work for a decent wage. The supportive services provided also have been helpful. Needless to say, many problems have not been solved, such as more effective recruitment, job placement, and followup on employers' pledges of jobs.

The JOBS program has succeeded in providing employment for people formerly thought to be unemployable, and, more importantly, because it has reached only a fraction of those needing help, more help is promised for the future. The training programs provided by JOBS not only provide current employment, but unproductive citizens of the past have been turned into permanently productive members of the labor force. This also raises the national income even more by increasing aggregate demand and providing a better labor force. Moreover, there is some spillover from JOBS programs into the regular training programs of the companies involved, leading to improvements.

Job Corps

The JOBS Program, in addition to replacing much effort formerly put into MDTA-OJT programs, will supplant many Job Corps programs. Whether this is a sound development remains to be seen. The Job Corps has taken underprivileged youths coming from a disadvantaged environment and provided entré to a more productive life. The Job Corps differs from other institutional training programs in that it is a residential program. Its members live at the Job Corps centers and are, hopefully, taught an entirely different way of life. In addition to basic education and training, they are introduced to many aspects of American life they have never known— such as an occasional meal at a decent restaurant. Many of the trainees have lost hope and are greatly in need of an introduction to the "decent" side of life. Many blacks would quarrel with the concept herein expressed which finds white middle-class values desirable, rejecting cultural patterns coming from the ghetto.

Corps members are, on the average, 17.5 years old, having completed nine years of school, but read and compute at the fifth-grade level. Sixty-three per cent of those eligible for the Job Corps do not meet the physical or educational standards for military service. In 1968, 59 per cent of the members were black.

Prior to the shutdown of fifty-five Job Corps centers in the spring of 1969, the Corps served 33,000 youths in 109 centers. Eighty-two of the centers were Job Corps Civilian Conservation Centers ostensibly serving young men least equipped for advanced vocational training. While the inductees engage in conservation work, these centers provide prevocational training and remedial education. The appraised value of the conservation work performed by the Conservation Centers at the end of 1968 was over $56 million.[430]

Politicians are understandably enthusiastic about having the conservation work accomplished in their districts, often without enthusiastically supporting the program. Unfortunately, the conservation centers do not teach skills necessary to earn a decent wage. The centers are concerned with conservation and keeping young men out of trouble while the provision for useful training and education is secondary. The Job Corps urban centers, more valuable to society in the long run than the conservation camps, have not been enthusiastically received by Congress.

The six men's and eighteen women's centers located near urban communities each provide the equivalent of a high school education and make available skill training in eleven basic types of vocations. Each type of program provides transferable skills, giving enrollees as much job mobility as possible. Unfortunately, these centers lack pork barrel appeal and many residents of the locality are upset by the "undesirable types" (due to color, lack of education, poverty, police records, etc.).

Despite benefiting by education and skill, Corps members have experienced trouble finding work when returning to the job market, leading to severe criticism of the program. While much of the criticism is justified, especially the relevance of the training in the conservation centers, a number of factors must be considered in evaluating the Job Corps.

In the first place, the Job Corps has only been in operation a few years; errors and inefficient programming were inevitable and correction and implementation have been undertaken. The many failures do not mean that the Job Corps is a complete waste of resources if successes can be eventually reported. To expect immediate success is, to say the least, unrealistic. Community hostility also damaged the centers.

The unemployment rate of those leaving the Job Corps is high: in June, 1968, approximately 30 per cent were not constructively occupied (63 per cent were employed and 7 per cent returned to school).[431] However, these figures include inductees dropping out after a short period in the program, and there has been a significant improvement over pre-Job Corps status when only 44 per cent held jobs. Among the former Job Corps members still unemployed, about one in four claimed an inability to find work because of a lack of transportation, and the same 25 per cent mentioned racial discrimination as the work deterrent.

According to the same survey, the average earnings of Job Corps graduates are substantially higher than before. Forty-four per cent working before entry into the Job Corps averaged $1.27 per hour. Corps members completing the program averaged $1.80 per hour one year after leaving the centers while earning $1.92 per hour in eighteen months. Even those spending less than three months in the Corps averaged $1.54 per hour one year later. While these earnings are still well below average, they represent a significant improvement.

Some benefit-cost analysis has been made for the Job Corps, indicating that benefits exceed cost. Studies show benefits exceeding cost by as much as five-to-one or as little as two-to-one, depending upon the assumptions used in the calculations.[132] Furthermore, many people assume that there will be no cost to society if the program is discontinued. Such an analysis of the Job Corps is clearly invalid. If enrollees fail to enter the mainstream of American life, many will undoubtedly cost society as much each year for the rest of their lives as one year in the Job Corps or any other manpower program. Thirty-three per cent of the Job Corps members have some kind of police record; many of them will undoubtedly spend years behind bars. Each such year will cost the taxpayer more than a year in the Job Corps. Similar conclusions can be reached if the costs for public welfare are calculated.

Many benefits cannot be quantified but may prove significant for many individuals. The benefit of becoming functionally literate exceeds the increased wages which one can earn. The isolation and frustration of a person unable to read and write or follow simple written instructions is difficult for most of us to understand. Too much emphasis has been placed on the expenditure of Job Corps funds to take trainees to dinners in good restaurants. Yet, this is part of modern living they have never seen, unless working as a busboy. To many people, the Job Corps represents success if it can restore hope and dignity to the downtrodden, regardless of the benefit-cost analysis.

Neighborhood Youth Corps

The Neighborhood Youth Corps (NYC) is a work-training program for youths which follows the goals and methods of the Job Corps without removing trainees from their home environment. Most of the participants are not as disadvantaged as Job Corps members. The NYC Program has three separate components with somewhat different objectives:

1) A program for youth of high school age who are in school, but not necessarily high school.
2) An out-of-school program.
3) A summer program designed to encourage high school students and drop-outs to return to school in the fall.[433]

The objective of the in-school program is to make it easier for enrollees to remain in school by providing financial assistance through part-time work. The enrollees are paid $1.25 per hour up to fifteen hours per week. These earnings may relieve some of the financial pressures which drive young people out of school. Over 200,000 were served by this NYC program in the fiscal year 1968; more than one-third of the enrollees came from families of eight persons or more, indicating the need for financial assistance.

More than 160,000 were enrolled in the out-of-school program during 1968, with blacks accounting for 45.2 per cent.[434] This program encourages the resumption of education and furnishes work experience in preparation for the competitive job market. In addition to paid work up to forty hours per week, out-of-school programs provide supportive services, including remedial education, counseling, and medical assistance. Compensation is currently being paid for time spent while receiving supportive services, if within the forty-hour week, to overcome resistance to participation in supportive activities on the trainees' time.

A recent study indicated that the NYC out-of-school program has not been as beneficial as anticipated.[435] It showed that former enrollees did not have a lower unemployment rate nor did they return to school in larger proportions than the control group of non-NYC enrollees. The findings suggested that the program should be strengthened with closer links between training and the industrial job market, more effective techniques developed for motivating return to school, and more emphasis placed on remedial education. Despite the failure of the out-of-school program to live up to expectations, some success has been reported as a few individual projects have worked well.

The summer NYC program is an attempt to provide work and sufficient money to permit young people to return to school. During the summer of 1968, 364,000 participated in this program and approximately 40 per cent were black.[436]

The majority of the youths participating in NYC programs are prime candidates for a life of poverty, crime, and unemployment. More than a fourth of all enrollees are on the welfare rolls or come from families receiving public assistance. The NYC has been credited with decreases in juvenile crime rates. In San Antonio, the crime rate dropped 12.6 per cent in the low-income areas where NYC was in operation, while climbing 5.5 per cent in the higher-income sections.[437] Only one per cent of 2,000 enrollees in Los Angeles had been convicted of crime since joining the project, though half of them entered with criminal records.[438]

New Careers Program

A relatively smallscale manpower program aimed at the disadvantaged and blacks in particular is the New Careers program. It prepares disadvantaged adults to hold subprofessional jobs, taking away some of the burden from the professional in public or private nonprofit agencies, operating in such undermanned fields as health, education, welfare, neighborhood redevelopment, and public safety. A significant amount of classroom training is involved in this program either before employment or during on-the-job training. The agencies providing the training guarantee jobs for enrollees after training is completed.

In 1968, approximately 5,000 persons were enrolled in New Careers projects. The median age was 31.5 years, the median annual family income was $1,934, and 73.9 per cent were black. The typical biographical data showed underemployment; 83.8 per cent worked sixteen to forty hours per week on their last job, earning about $1.30 per hour.[439]

The emphasis in the program is on the individual already in the labor force unable to progress economically. The program is small and it is too early to judge its viability. The agencies involved have not always performed adequately, and, as always, more supportive services are needed. One major problem has been excessively rigid state and local civil service or merit system requirements; the formal educational requirements for many public jobs have effectively barred blacks capable of doing the work. Private industry has begun to relax hiring standards in order to employ the disadvantaged, and similar steps will have to be taken by state and local governments. But there is political opposition from those opposed to helping blacks and others. Also, since many civil service systems have been carefully constructed over the years to separate politics from public employment, many fear the relaxation of standards.

Operation Mainstream

Operation Mainstream provides job opportunities for chronically unemployed adults unable to find jobs due to age or lack of skill. Work experience is provided for the trainees while skill training, basic education, counseling, and other supportive services are added. Meanwhile, the trainees are employed to beautify and improve community projects operated by public and nonprofit agencies. The projects are primarily located in small communities and rural areas.

There were about 200 Operation Mainstream projects in 1968.[440] In 1967 and 1968, approximately 24,000 disadvantaged adults were enrolled. The median age was 49.7 years; 25.4 per cent were blacks. The median years of schooling was 8.0, and median annual family income was $1,759. Eighty-one per cent worked between sixteen and forty hours per week on their last job, earning about $1.45 per hour. Thirty per cent were on welfare rolls immediately before enrollment. Clearly, the apparent cost of $45.9 million of Operation Mainstream for 1967 and 1968 is greater than the real cost, considering the reduction in welfare and unemployment payments. Many enrollees are enthusiastic about the program and more than one-third have found regular jobs as a result of the skills acquired. It has been recommended that separate projects be set up for enrollees who can be expected to move into the competitive job market and for others who cannot. For the latter group, long-time subsidization may be required.

Special Impact Program

The Special Impact Program (SIP) focuses on specific neighborhoods with large numbers of poor people. The purpose is to develop new skills, entrepreneurship, opportunities, and improvements sufficiently conspicuous to arrest community tensions. Essentially, the program will promote economic, business, and community development.

SIP funds are not to be spread thinly over numerous projects. The $24.3 million obligated in 1967 went to programs in blighted areas in major cities, including the Bedford-Stuyvesant area, the largest ghetto in the country.[441] In 1968, $20 million went to support programs in Watts and other ghetto and rural areas, including the Bedford-Stuyvesant project. Some SIP funds also went to support JOBS projects.

SIP projects are used to encourage private enterprise to establish facilities in or near ghettos so as to provide employment and train the "untrainable." Expenses incurred in training and in providing supportive services are covered by contract agreements, which may run as long as thirty months, negotiated by the firm and federal government.

In addition to employing and training the hard core, SIP encourages local entrepreneurship and promotes the total economic development of the neighborhood. Thus, its reach is beyond problems pertaining to manpower and reaches the entire economy of the area. For example, a grant may be made to a community corporation founded by area residents. The corporation then finances and provides technical assistance to firms owned and operated by area residents; it may also develop a business or community service.

130

Once again, it is too early to evaluate the results of this program as economic development does not take place overnight. The Bedford-Stuyvesant program has been operating longer than any other SIP project, and positive results have only recently been claimed for it. In Bedford-Stuyvesant, employment has been provided for 1,300 considered to be hard-core unemployed. As of January, 1969, SIP received forty-six proposals for new or extended business operations and approved fourteen. A Community Home Improvement program has renovated the exteriors of eleven blocks in Bedford-Stuyvesant and is progressing on twelve more blocks.[442]

Work Incentive Program

There have been several attempts to encourage people on welfare to seek gainful employment, such as the Community Work and Training Program in 1962, the Work-Experience Program in 1964, and the Work-Experience and Training Program in 1966. Minimal funding was provided for these programs so that only a small number on welfare rolls was reached. In 1967, the Work Incentive Program (WIN) set as a national goal the restoration of economic independence of all employable persons over sixteen years of age in families receiving Aid to Families with Dependent Children (AFDC). All states were required to enter WIN by July 1, 1969.[443]

In WIN, an individual remains on the welfare roles after obtaining his first job until his ability to support himself is established. WIN currently has a very small appropriation, but the authorizing legislation is open-ended. The Manpower Administration claims that Congress will provide enough money, eventually, to reach all those on AFDC (currently 1.4 million people). The philosophy behind this program is much the same as that behind the negative income tax. Referrals by welfare agencies to WIN manpower services proceed under three priorities geared to ability to enter the job market. Priority I is given to people who are judged job-ready when entering the program. Attempts are made to find them on-the-job training, and supportive services are also available. Trainees are allowed to keep the first $30 of their monthly earnings plus 30 per cent of all additional earnings, without losing welfare benefits. For example, a person earning $100 per week could keep $51 of his salary plus his welfare income. This approach approximates the negative income tax proposals.

Individuals who are not job-ready, but who are trainable through work orientation, basic education, skill training, and work experience, are placed in priority II. Intensive efforts are made to persuade employers to hire these individuals while supportive services are provided. During the training period, $30 per month is added to welfare benefits as a training incentive.

Priority III is assigned to those who are not ready to undertake the training given to trainees in priority II. Special work projects are arranged with public or private nonprofit agencies to keep them occupied. The ability to move to a higher priority is reviewed every three months. Participants in Priority III are guaranteed that their income will equal their welfare payments plus $20.

Only $10 million was appropriated for WIN in the fiscal year 1968, which cared for 8,200 enrollees in eleven states. The $118 million appropriated for the fiscal year 1969 will support about 100,000 enrollees as well as provide day-care services for some of their children.[444] Data on the racial composition of those participating in WIN are not available, but many blacks have enrolled.

United States Employment Service

It should be obvious from the above listing of manpower programs that the task of coordinating them is an extremely difficult one. One logical agency to implement manpower policy is the United States Employment Service with its many state and local branches. However, to fill this role, basic changes—a redefinition of mission and a redirection of effort—were necessary. Before 1962, the Employment Service was primarily a labor exchange and administered work tests to those claiming unemployment insurance, offering help to job seekers and employers. The role of the Service was broadened to identify people needing employment assistance, to match people to jobs, and to develop a structure free of discrimination and discourage unnecessary hiring requirements. Funds for the Employment Service more than doubled from 1967 to 1968 (to $341 million) to broaden services; the number of local offices were increased by one-fourth (to 2,147); and the Human Resources Development (HRD) concept was developed.[445] Since these offices are state controlled, some states have been considerably more sincere and successful in accomplishing this than others.

To implement HRD concepts, all Employment Service efforts are brought together to serve better those facing employment difficulties. HRD recognizes that special effort must be made to seek out the disadvantaged and the logical starting point is the identification of those needing help.

The second basic premise of HRD is that the disadvantaged need special kinds of services to prepare them for regular employment. These services include special counseling and listing, instructions in adjusting to industrial discipline, occupational training referrals, and continuing contact with the worker after he is gainfully employed. In addition, the understanding of employers hiring these disadvantaged workers is sought.

Concentrated Employment Program

The drive to improve the coordination of manpower programming has led to the development of services which enable individuals to get help to

132

solve their employment problems. One such system is the Concentrated Employment Program (CEP), designed to combine individual manpower programs into a comprehensive system of services in the urban slum neighborhoods and impoverished rural areas. CEP coordinates a plethora of programs through central funding, avoiding duplication and providing necessary supportive services tailored to the individual need of the trainee.[446]

There were seventy-six CEP's in operation by late 1968, of which thirteen were located in rural areas. The urban sites were selected for CEP on the basis of the severity of underemployment and local capability to support a CEP. Rural area selection was based upon need and the potential for economic growth. The existence of other federal programs related to the CEP has also been an additional factor in site selection.

A total of 118,000 people had been interviewed for CEP admission by late September, 1968. Of these, 38,000 were placed in regular employment, while 23,000 have completed their basic education or other institutional training programs.[447] Eight per cent of the CEP enrollees have been black; 20 per cent were on welfare, and half of them were unemployed for at least fifteen weeks in the year prior to their enrollment.

The CEP usually is sponsored by the local Community Action Agency (CAA), which, with other agencies, plans for and implements the CEP. The Employment Service, under the direction of the CAA, ordinarily provides the basic services needed by CEP clients to find and hold jobs. The other kinds of services—basic education, skill training, and some supportive services—are supplied by a variety of local institutions. These include public schools, junior colleges, and relevant federal programs, such as NYC or JOBS.

To inspire CEP receptivity and assure the fulfillment of local needs, local participation is stressed. A directive has been issued requiring that half the staff of a newly established CEP reside in the neighborhood.

While the CEP is to provide order and central direction to manpower programs, this goal has not yet been accomplished. The supply of jobs for CEP enrollees is inadequate because few employers are involved in the program.[448] CEP sponsors have been unable to gain the confidence of large firms capable of hiring the disadvantaged. The failure to win over the large firm is partially due to local control of the CEP and the CAA. Those participating in CEP have not been able to, or have not tried to, gain the respect of the local business and political leaders. Their mutual distrust is a major obstacle to successful programs in slums and ghettos.

Neighborhood Services Pilot Program

The Neighborhood Services Pilot Program (NSPP) was started in 1966 to establish neighborhood centers in the ghettos. The centers are to provide job information and training as well as health, education, recreation, and other community services. A committee from HUD decided that demonstration programs should be initiated in fourteen cities. Three possible kinds of centers were suggested—an advice and job referral center, a diagnostic and limited service center, and a one-stop service center for all services. Plans for centers in thirteen cities have been approved and funds allocated.[449]

Since the start of NSPP, both the CEP and the Model Cities Program were introduced. In twelve of the fourteen cities, the NSPP and CEP operations are adjacent; efforts are being made to coordinate NSPP with CEP and Model Cities where possible. There are no data on black involvement in NSPP, but given the tie-in with CEP and Model Cities, some benefit to the black is likely.

Model Cities Program

The Model Cities Program was legislatively authorized in 1966 to provide for the rebuilding of cities and uplift the living conditions of the urban resident.[450] Basic to the rebuilding program is the provision for manpower services. HUD has been assigned overall responsibility for this program, but OEO, HEW, and the Department of Labor are also involved.

Planning grants have been made to seventy-five cities and operation was scheduled by summer, 1969. A substantial number of these cities have large black populations and many of the specific projects will upgrade black neighborhoods.

The manpower programs of the federal government have helped many blacks and other disadvantaged workers in the United States, but much remains to be done. Many blacks have not yet been reached and others require additional assistance. The evaluation of past or existing programs and future programs will be now undertaken in three parts: financial, organizational, and services provided.

Obviously, the manpower program will require more money. While there has been waste and inefficiency, even the best of programs will need considerably more financial assistance. But there is public opposition to financial sponsorship that is both practical and ideological. Many people feel that it is wasteful to support some lazy slob, especially a black one, without ambition to finish school. It should be obvious that the authors do not have much sympathy for this point of view.

Some feel that a meaningful manpower program will cost too much and that we cannot afford it. Refuting this rationale is relatively simple, since it is based on economic rather than ideological factors. The truth of the matter is that we must finance adequate manpower programs. Benefit-cost analysis indicates that many programs more than return their cost. Earlier, estimation of lost GNP due to underemployment was provided. Providing minimal public assistance payments or supporting penal institutions may be more costly than providing the necessary training and supportive services given to program trainees.

In the short run, taxes will be higher to mount a meaningful manpower program than if no commitment were made. However, in the long run, society will benefit financially and otherwise. And this is true if one considers only the pecuniary aspect of welfare. The real income (money income corrected for taxes and price changes) of most people will be higher because the need for public assistance will drop and the contribution made to the gross national product by those currently underemployed and their families will increase.

If the nonpecuniary aspects of welfare are considered, most Americans will benefit even more. Most of us feel some guilt, anger, or sorrow because of the black "problem" and other disadvantaged individuals.

There is no doubt that manpower programs from the organizational viewpoint have been the cause of much despair. The number of programs discussed makes it obvious that serious organizational problems are encountered. Part of this is related to the political environment and the difficulty of getting appropriations. Part is due to the experimentation necessary to develop adequate training programs and supportive services.

It appears that more programs will be coordinated but at the local or community level. Hopefully, local control will be exercised in a manner which will earn the respect of the power structure in the area. Both coordination and local involvement are necessary to successful programming.

As manpower programs in the United States developed during the 1960s, it was necessary to provide services not originally envisioned. Training in a particular skill is not enough to help slum residents. Training alone may be enough for those with a satisfactory basic education or who have shown ability to hold a job in the past. Others need much more: basic education, counseling, development of new attitudes, etc. Beyond this, the development of community facilities and business is necessary. In many ways, the problems in the ghettos are the same as in underdeveloped countries, such as an inadequate infrastructure (transportation, public services, etc.), few businesses with large capital investment, even fewer which keep the profits in the underdeveloped area, and a labor force unable to meet the standards of twentieth century industrialization. Few are skilled, many are poorly educated, and few can match the standards of behavior imposed by modern business. It takes time for an individual to learn to report to work daily and on time and to submit to industrial dicipline. To break the cycle of poverty and underemployment which has trapped so many blacks requires more than is currently known of manpower programming. But manpower programs are an integral part of the total task which must be coordinated with other elements. Even if programs are adequately funded and efficiently operated, differences between black and white income can only be slowly eliminated. Perhaps more dramatic projects are necessary in the short run to supply the uplifting that is absolutely essential.

CHAPTER ELEVEN ✖ EPILOGUE

The current economic state of the black is directly attributable to religious, economic, political, and juridical thought formulated prior to and after the Civil War. All influential segments within the United States would have had to make an all-out effort to squelch racial discrimination before the black could have made a satisfactory transition from slavery to freedom. Government indifference and the prevailing economic and legal thought of the nineteenth and twentieth centuries helped to keep the black in a state that was not far removed from slavery. Neutrality, laissez faire, the cure-all time, none of these stock cures could contain the racial prejudices so prevalent throughout the nation.

Perhaps even worse than indifference, given differing labels and explanations, was the sweeping under the carpet of the extent to which racial prejudice was a part of our heritage. Grammar school, high school, and even universities put forth an image of tolerance in the United States that was untrue. This was unfortunate because cures are not undertaken until the illness is diagnosed. Even today, blacks are held responsible for their economic and social failures by much of the white community.

The assumption of greater responsibility by the federal government for black welfare started, unintentionally, during the 1930 depression with the birth of Keynesian economics. Because of executive intervention before and after World War II, there was a possible "multiplier effect" in government, leading to a philosophical shift in the decision-making of the Supreme Court. From the end of World War II to the present, the Supreme Court has been a champion of what is broadly termed "civil rights." While the Supreme Court does not face the political pressures of the executive and legislative branches of government, it was, nevertheless, in tune with the need for change. Unfortunately, many of the executive and subsequent legislative responses to the needs of the black community came grudgingly, after the use of revolutionary and violent tactics. The black is convinced that change only follows violence.

Government, business, and union leaders could aid substantially the black quest for fair employment; all that would be necessary is a shifting of emphasis from the solving of technical problems to extending meaningful aid to the black. But it would require a resolution that is, for the most part, missing. While much of the emphasis today with respect to fair employment is on the black, perhaps as much or more emphasis should be placed on the white community. Certainly a better job can be done in presenting the black point of view and educating the white community. Not only must the white community assume current responsibility for black welfare but the extent to which prejudice has been practiced should be highlighted. Too many in our society, educators included, are uninterested in assuming responsibility for the patterns of prejudice that have developed over the years. Without dedication and resolution there can be no end to racial strife. There is some doubt in the minds of the authors as to whether all-out attempts to contain racial prejudice will be completely successful, but certainly some success can be anticipated.

With an all-out effort to end discrimination, many of the white-black problems can be resolved in several generations. Without dedicated resolution, the same patterns of hatred, violence, and deprivation will continue generation after generation. It is evident today that a considerable percentage of our white society is not convinced that Herculean efforts are necessary to effectuate meaningful changes.

The black does not feel grateful, nor should he, for the limited and grudging effort made since World War II in his behalf. The black wants and is entitled to exactly the same kind of economic and social treatment that is given to the white. What is difficult is that the black has a lot of catching-up to do before he can be an equal of the white.

The black community must be convinced of the good faith of his white brethren. Perhaps our greatest hope lies in the younger person who is less likely to be prejudiced than the older person.[451]

FOOTNOTES ⚏

1. F. Fanon, *The Wretched of the Earth*, pp. 20-21 (paperback, 1968).

2. A. W. Lind, *Race Relations in World Perspective*, pp. 67-70 (1955).

3. More than 70 per cent of the black population live in urban centers.

4. The National Commission on Urban Problems, *The Challenging of America's Metropolitan Population Outlook—1960 to 1985*, Research Rept. No. 3, p. 19 (1968).

5. *Id.*, p. 21.

6. *Id.*, p. 25.

7. Colegrove v. Green, 328 U.S. 549 (1946); Baker v. Carr, 369 U.S. 186 (1962); Reynolds v. Sims, 377 U.S. 533 (1964).

8. A. Meier and E. M. Rudwick, *From Plantation to Ghetto*, pp. 10-11 (1966).

9. J. H. Franklin, *From Slavery to Freedom*, pp. 34-38 (1950).

10. As used here, geometric expression refers to the use of straight lines, circles, and triangles as artistic forms.

11. H. Read, *A Concise History of Modern Painting*, pp. 69-70 (paperback 1959).

12. L. Bennett, *Before the Mayflower. . . . : A History of the Negro in America*, pp. 23-25 (1962).

13. J. H. Franklin, *From Slavery to Freedom*, pp. 7-8.

14. *Id.*, pp. 42-43.

15. J. F. Bell, *A History of Economic Thought*, p. 15 (2nd ed., 1967).

16. *Theaetatus* 175a

17. Moore, *The Roman's World*, pp. 65-75 (1936); Moore, *The Roman Commonwealth*, pp. 102-103 (1942).

18. R. N. Sherwin-White, *Racial Prejudice in Imperial Rome*, pp. 17-21, 64-65, 86-87, 96 (1967).

19. *Democracy in America*, Vol. 1, p. 395 (paperback, 1954).

20. H. Maine, *Ancient Law*, pp. 156-161 (paperback, 1963).

21. *Id.*, pp. 159-161.

22. W. Walsh, *A History of Anglo-American Law*, pp. 23-24 (paperback, 2nd ed., 1950).

23. J. H. Franklin, *From Slavery to Freedom*, pp. 44-46.

24. O. Handlin, *Race and Nationality in American Life*, pp. 4-5 (paperback, 1957).

25. F. J. Brown and J. S. Roucek, *One America*, pp. 29-30 (1945); J. H. Franklin, *From Slavery to Freedom*, pp. 46-49.

26. Ottley, *Black Odyssey*, p. 16 (1950).

27. J. H. Franklin, *From Slavery to Freedom*, pp. 49-57.

28. G. Freyre, *The Masters and the Slaves*, A Study in the Development of Brazilian Civilization, p. 4 (1956).

29. *Op. cit.*, pp. 118-121.

30. *Op. cit.*, pp. 281, 298-299.

31. *Id.*, pp. 81, 299, 307.

32. M. R. Konvitz and T. Leskes, *A Century of Civil Rights*, pp. 26-32 (1961).

33. R. N. Sherwin-White, *Racial Prejudice in Imperial Rome*, pp. 93-94.

34. Using the Jew as an example of discrimination is questionable; much of the dis-

crimination practiced against the Jew was fanned by Christianity, a competing religion.

35. The Jew is also an example of this type of discrimination.

36. Ginzberg, "American Democracy and the Negro," in *The Negro Challenge to the Business Community*, pp. 2-3 (paperback, 1964); Ottley, *Black Odyssey*, pp. 6-7.

37. Johnson, "Changing Status of the Negro in American Life," 1 *Journal of Intergroup Relations* 56, 57 (Spring, 1960).

38. F. R. Dulles, *Labor in America*, p. 3 (1966).

39. A. Craven, *The Coming of the Civil War*, pp. 70-71 (1942).

40. E. T. Thompson, *Race Relations and the Race Problem*, see Reuter, "Competition and the Racial Division of Labor," p. 55 (1939).

41. O. Handlin, *Race and Nationality in American Life*, pp. 12-26.

42. Russel, "The Economic History of Negro Slavery in the United States," 11 *Agricultural History* 308 (1937).

43. Jenkins, *Pro-Slavery Thought in the Old South*, p. 3 (1935).

44. J. H. Franklin, *From Slavery to Freedom*, pp. 70-71.

45. O. Handlin, *Race and Nationality in American Life*, pp. 18-19.

46. A. W. Lind, *Race Relations in World Perspective*, see A. F. Frazier, "The Negro in the United States," pp. 341-348.

47. J. H. Franklin, *From Slavery to Freedom*, pp. 95-99.

48. H. W. Spiegel, *The Rise of American Economic Thought*, p. 10 (1952).

49. *Id.*, pp. 20-21.

50. J. H. Franklin, *From Slavery to Freedom*, p. 145.

51. Litwack, *North of Slavery*, pp. 3-4 (1961).

52. *Id.*, pp. 3-15.

53. A. Craven, *The Coming of the Civil War*, pp. 100-102.

54. 3 and 4 Will. IV, Ch. 73.

55. 47 Geo. III, Ch. 36; 51 Geo. III, Ch. 23.

56. J. F. Normano, *The Spirit of American Economics*, p. 79 (1943).

57. Grimes, *Equality in America*, p. 45 (1964).

58. C. A. Beard, *An Economic Interpretation of the Constitution of the United States*, pp. 29-30 (paperback, 1961).

59. *Democracy in America*, Vol. 1, p. 370.

60. *Id.*, p. 373.

61. *Id.*, p. 390.

62. A. P. Grimes, *Equality in America*, p. 27.

63. A. Meier and E. M. Rudwick, *From Plantation to Ghetto*, p. 15 (1966).

64. L. Pope, *The Kingdom Beyond Caste*, pp. 21-22 (1957).

65. *Id.*, pp. 22-27.

66. H. S. Commager, *Freedom and Order*, p. 47 (1966).

67. Jenkins, *Pro-Slavery Thought in the Old South*, pp. 6-10 (1935).

68. E. T. Thompson, *Race Relations and the Race Problem*, see C. S. Johnson, "Race Relations And Social Change," p. 281.

69. E. F. Frazier, *The Negro in the United States*, p. 24 (1966).

70. Meier and Rudwick, *From Plantation to Ghetto*, pp. 74-76.

71. Ross, *Slavery Ordained of God* (1857); Armstrong, *The Christian Doctrine of Slavery* (1857).

72. L. Lomax, *When the Word Is Given . . .*, pp. 41-42 (1963).

73. Jenkins, *Pro-Slavery Thought in the Old South*, pp. 17-20.

74. J. H. Franklin, *From Slavery to Freedom*, p. 104.

75. *Op. cit.*, pp. 208-209.

76. Everson v. Bd. of Education, 330 U.S. 1 (1947); McCollum v. Bd. of Education,

333 U.S. 203 (1948); Zorach v. Clauson, 343 U.S. 306 (1952); Engle v. Vitale, 370 U.S. 421 (1962).

77. J. M. McPherson, *The Struggle for Equality*, p. 5 (1964).

78. Hill, "Southern Protestanism and Racial Integration," in McDonagh and Simpson, *Social Problems: Persistent Challenges*, pp. 342-344 (paperback, 1966). This study was made in Little Rock, Arkansas.

79. R. B. Nye, *Fettered Freedom*, pp. 181-182 (1963).

80. R. H. Tawney, *Religion and the Rise of Capitalism*, pp. 92-101 (1962).

81. *Id.*, pp. 184-185.

82. M. Weber, *The Protestant Ethic and the Spirit of Capitalism*, pp. 84-85 (1948).

83. *Op. cit.*, pp. 269-271.

84. *Op. cit.*, pp. 98-105.

85. *Id.*, pp. 55-56.

86. J. H. Franklin, *From Slavery to Freedom*, pp. 108, 176-177.

87. *Black's Law Dictionary*, 3rd ed.

88. J. H. Franklin, *From Slavery to Freedom*, p. 108.

89. *Id.*, pp. 176-177.

90. Simpson and Yinger, *Racial and Cultural Minorities*, p. 405.

91. Editors of Ebony, article entitled "The Un-Christian Christian," *The White Problem in America*, p. 61 (1966).

92. Faulkner, *American Economic History*, p. 314 (1960). Also see data at footnote 60.

93. Batchelder, *The Economics of Poverty*, p. 34 (1966).

94. *Id.*, p. 34.

95. Cipolla, *The Economic History of World Population*, p. 47 (1962).

96. *Wealth of Nations* (1937).

97. Roll, *A History of Economic Thought*, p. 35 (1959).

98. *Essay on Population* (1927).

99. Ricardo, *Principles of Political Economy and Taxation* (1957).

100. Gill, *Evolution of Modern Economics*, p. 23 (1967).

101. Phillips, *American Negro Slavery* (1933).

102. Conrad and Meyer, "The Economics of Slavery in the Ante-Bellum South," 66 *Journal of Political Economy* 95-130 (1958)

103. Profit, as used here, means that the rate of return on investment in slaves was higher than the average rate of return on all investments in the economy.

104. Dowd, "The Economics of Slavery in the Ante-Bellum South: A Comment," 66 *Journal of Political Economy* 440-442 (1958)

105. Easterlin, "Regional Income Trends, 1840-1950," in Harris, *American Economic History*, p. 528 (1961).

106. Stephenson, *Race Distinctions in American Law*, p. 7 (1910).

107. Maitland, "The Deacon and the Jewess; Or, Apostasy at Common Law," 2 *Law Quarterly Rev.* 153 (1886).

108. Litwack, *North of Slavery*, pp. 31-39.

109. *Id.*, pp. 46-47.

110. *Id.*, pp. 156-157.

111. J. H. Franklin, *From Slavery to Freedom*, pp. 196-197.

112. R. B. Nye, *Fettered Freedom*, p. 144.

113. *An Economic Interpretation of the Constitution of the United States*, pp. 29-30.

114. S. Lynd, *Class Conflict, Slavery and the United States Constitution*, pp. 18-19 (1967).

115. Ginzberg and Eichner, *The Troublesome Presence; American Democracy and the Negro*, pp. 67-69 (1964).

141

116. U.S. Riot Commission Report, *Report of the National Advisory Commission on Civil Disorders*, p. 208 (1968).

117. J. H. Franklin, *From Slavery to Freedom*, pp. 127-129.

118. S. Lynd, *Class Conflict, Slavery and the United States Constitution*, pp. 3-5.

119. Ottley, *Black Odyssey*, pp. 74-75.

120. *Op. cit.*, p. 173.

121. Moes, "The Absorption of Capital in Slave Labor in the Ante-Bellum South and Economic Growth," 20 *American Journal of Economics and Sociology* 535 (1961).

122. Konvitz and Leskes, *A Century of Civil Rights*, p. 17.

123. J. H. Franklin, *From Slavery to Freedom*, pp. 73-79.

124. Stephenson, *Race Distinctions in American Law*, pp. 38-39.

125. *Op. cit.*, p. 205.

126. R. B. Nye, *Fettered Freedom*, pp. 1-3.

127. *Id.*, pp. 13-15.

128. Salsbury, "The Effect of the Civil War on American Industrial Development," in Andreano, *The Economic Impact of the American Civil War*, pp. 161-163.

129. Ottley, *Black Odyssey*, pp. 42-44.

130. Johnson, "Changing Status of the Negro in American Life," 1 *Journal of Intergroup Relations* 56 (1960).

131. S. Lynd, *Class Conflict, Slavery and the United States Constitution*, p. 181.

132. Litwack, *North of Slavery*, pp. 275-277.

133. Ginzberg and Eichner, *The Troublesome Presence; American Democracy and the Negro*, pp. 105-106.

134. Woodward, *The Strange Career of Jim Crow*, p. 21 (paperback, 1966).

135. T. H. Williams, *Lincoln and the Radicals*, p. 5 (1941).

136. *Id.*, pp. 309-311.

137. J. M. McPherson, *The Struggle for Equality*, p. 11.

138. *Id.*, pp. 107-108.

139. *Id.*, p. 155. This failed and Lincoln sent a ship to Haiti to bring the blacks back.

140. *Id.*, pp. 193-196.

141. T. H. Williams, *Lincoln and the Radicals*, pp. 335-377.

142. R. B. Nye, *Fettered Freedom*, pp. 91-109.

143. Coppage v. Kansas, 236 U.S. 1 (1915); Adair v. U.S., 208 U.S. 161 (1908).

144. *The Economic Mind in American Civilization*, Vol. III (1949).

145. Ginzberg, "American Democracy and the Negro," *The Negro Challenge to the Business Community*, p. 7.

146. J. M. McPherson, *The Struggle for Equality*, pp. 246-247. Unfortunately, abolitionists pushed for land ownership for the black rather than training for industry.

147. *Id.*, pp. 213-241.

148. G. R. Bentley, *A History of the Freedmen's Bureau*, p. 39 (1955).

149. B. T. Washington, *The Story of the Negro: The Rise of the Race from Slavery*, Vol. II, p. 114 (1940).

150. *Op. cit.*, p. 89.

151. P. S. Peirce, *The Freedmen's Bureau*, pp. 129-132 (1904). Published by the State University of Iowa, Studies in Sociology, Economics, Politics and History, Vol. III, No. 1.

152. *Id.*, pp. 132-133.

153. Ginzberg and Eichner, *The Troublesome Presence; American Democracy and the Negro*, p. 201. Private sources also contributed money and teachers to help educate the black.

154. Franklin, "History of Racial Segregation in the United States," 304 *The Annals* 1, 3-4 (1956).

155. G. R. Bentley, *A History of the Freedmen's Bureau*, pp. 62-63.

156. *Id.*, pp. 105-107.

157. Ginzberg and Eichner, *The Troublesome Presence; American Democracy and the Negro*, pp. 203-205.

158. *Op. cit.*, pp. 23-24.

159. E. F. Frazier, *The Negro in the United States*, pp. 114-122.

160. O. Handlin, *Race and Nationality in American Life*, p. 35.

161. C. V. Woodward, *The Strange Career of Jim Crow*, p. 85. By 1904, only 1,342 blacks registered as voters.

162. Bennett, *Before the Mayflower . . . : A History of the Negro in America*, pp. 183-186.

163. King and Quick, *Legal Aspects of the Civil Rights Movement*, pp. 10-11 (1965).

164. G. T. Stephenson, *Race Distinctions in American Law*, pp. 41-43.

165. Franklin, "History of Racial Segregation in the United States," 304 *The Annals* 1-3 (1956).

166. Ginzberg and Eichner, *The Troublesome Presence; American Democracy and the Negro*, pp. 212-215.

167. E. F. Frazier, *The Negro in the United States*, pp. 124-125.

168. J. M. McPherson, *The Struggle for Equality*, p. 317.

169. Ginzberg and Eichner, *The Troublesome Presence; American Democracy and the Negro*, pp. 150-151.

170. Simpson and Yinger, *Racial and Cultural Minorities*, p. 305.

171. H. Wish, *The Negro Since Emancipation*, p. 4 (1964).

172. Ginzberg and Eichner, *The Troublesome Presence; American Democracy and the Negro*, p. 273.

173. T. F. Gossett, *Race: The History of an Idea in America*, pp. 268-279 (paperback, 1965).

174. *Op. cit.*, pp. 272-274.

175. J. H. Franklin, *From Slavery to Freedom*, pp. 445-446.

176. T. F. Gossett, *Race: The History of an Idea in America*, p. 279.

177. Ginzberg and Eichner, *The Troublesome Presence; American Democracy and the Negro*, pp. 274-275.

178. Many lawyers and jurists claim that it is not the function of the Supreme Court to assume leadership in the moral sphere. But that is what the Supreme Court has been doing since World War II.

179. Bailey v. Alabama, 219 U.S. 219 (1911).

180. J. M. McPherson, *The Struggle for Equality*, pp. 126-127.

181. 392 U.S. 409 (1968).

182. Southern congressmen were absent while voting in Congress was underway.

183. Ten Broek, *Equal Under Law*, pp. 159-197 (1965).

184. *Id.*, p. 201.

185. 109 U.S. 3(1883).

186. G. Myers, *History of Bigotry in the United States*, pp. 210-258 (1943).

187. Epstein and Forster, *Some of My Best Friends*, . . . , pp. 5-6 (1962).

188. C. McWilliams, *Brothers Under the Skin*, pp. 89-92 (1951).

189. Simpson and Yinger, *Racial and Cultural Minorities*, pp. 93-98.

190. Ginzberg and Eichner, *The Troublesome Presence; Democracy and the Negro*, pp. 208-209.

191. E. F. Frazier, *The Negro in the United States,* pp. 159-162.

192. T. F. Gossett, *Race: The History of an Idea in America,* pp. 270-271.

193. Three civil rights workers were killed in Mississippi with the blessing of local gendarmes. See U.S. v. Price, 383 U.S. 787 (1966).

194. 109 U.S., at pp. 12-18.

195. Brown v. Mississippi, 297 U.S. 278 (1936).

196. NLRB v. Jones & Laughlin Steel Co., 301 U.S. 1 (1937).

197. Ten Broek, *Equal Under Law,* p. 119.

198. H. S. Commager, *Freedom and Order,* p. 190. Also see M. R. Konvitz, *Expanding Liberties,* pp. 12-13 (paperback, 1967).

199. 3 U.S.C., Title 12, Sec. 38 (1964 ed.).

200. 1 U.S.C., Title 1, Sec. 301.

201. 23 Stat. 3321.

202. 12 Stat. 392.

203. 12 Stat. 178.

204. 14 Stat. 251.

205. Scott v. Sandford, 60 U.S. 393 (1857).

206. Brown v. Bd. of Education, 347 U.S. 483.

207. 163 U.S. 537.

208. At footnote 205.

209. Litwack, *North of Slavery,* pp. 49-50.

210. Countryman, "The Constitution and Job Discrimination," 39 *Washington Law Review* 74, 75 (1964).

211. Civil Rights Cases, 109 U.S., at p. 25.

212. Ginzberg and Eichner, *The Troublesome Presence; American Democracy and the Negro,* p. 249.

213. "Legislation," 17 *University of Pittsburgh Law Review,* 439 (1956), *Third Annual Report* (Fair Employment, Indiana, 1956); Marrow, *Prejudice and Scientific Method in Labor Relations,* 5 *Industrial and Labor Relations Rev.* 593, 594 (1952).

214. H. R. Rep. No. 1370, 87th Cong. 2nd Sess., pp. 1-3 (1962).

215. Cochran, "Did The Civil War Retard Industrialization," in R. Andreano, *The Economic Impact of the American Civil War,* p. 155.

216. C. V. Woodward, *The Strange Career of Jim Crow,* p. 71.

217. Keynes, *The General Theory of Employment, Interest and Money* (1936).

218. *Id.,* pp. 194-209.

219. *Annual Report of the Council of Economic Advisers,* pp. 232, 305 (1969).

220. Blalock, "Occupational Discrimination: Some Theoretical Propositions," 9 *Social Problems* 240, 245-247 (1962).

221. F. Fanon, *Black Skin White Masks,* pp. 224-225 (1967).

222. Maslow, "FEPC—A Case History in Parliamentary Maneuver," 13 *University of Chicago Law Rev.* 407 (1946).

223. R. C. Weaver, *Negro Labor a National Problem,* pp. 18, 41-43 (1946).

224. *First Report Fair Employment Practices Comm. Rept.,* pp. 85-89 (1943-1944).

225. U.S. Riot Commission Rept., *Report of the National Advisory Commission on Civil Disorders,* pp. 5-16.

226. 14 Stat. 27.

227. 16 Stat. 140.

228. 16 Stat. 433.

229. 18 Stat. 336, *et al.*

230. Collins v. Hardyman, 341 U.S. 651 (1951); Corrigan v. Buckley, 271 U.S. 323 (1927); Hodges v. U.S., 203 U.S. 1 (1906); *Ex parte* Yarbrough, 110 U.S. 651 (1884);

144

U.S. v. Cruikshank, 92 U.S. 542 (1875); The Slaughter House Cases, 83 U.S. 36 (1872).

231. 18 U.S.C., Sec. 241, 242; 42 U.S.C., Sec. 1983 (1964); Screws v. U.S., 325 U.S. 91 (1945). The post Civil War legislation was inadequate to deal with the current problems because of vagueness, emphasis on criminal proceedings, and its intended limited effectiveness.

232. American Enterprise Institute for Public Policy Research, *Roles of the Attorney General of the United States*, see Dixon, "The Attorney General and Civil Rights 1870-1964," p. 111 (1968).

233. *Id.*, see Krislov, "The Role of the Attorney General as Amicus Curiae," p. 73.

234. Harper and Etherington, "Lobbyists Before the Court," 101 *University of Pennsylvania Law Rev.* 1172 (1953).

235. *Rules of the Supreme Court of the United States*, Rule 29 (June 12, 1967).

236. 42 U.S.C., Sec. 2000 e *et seq.*

237. "Role of Justice Department in Equal Job Opportunity," 68 *L.R.R.* 376 (8-12-68).

238. Sec. 707.

239. Kovarsky, "The Negro and Fair Employment," 56 *Kentucky Law Journal* 757, 795-800 (1968).

240. "NAM Summary Analysis of Revised OFCC Regulations," 68 *L.R.R.*, 190 (Vol. 68, No. 17, 7-1-68).

241. This requirement may conflict with section 703 (j) of Title VII which protects the employer unwilling to prefer blacks in hiring.

242. "Role of Justice Department in Equal Job Opportunity," 68 *L.R.R.* 376.

243. 29 *Fed. Reg.* 15569 (1964).

244. 31 *Fed. Reg.* 15024 (1966).

245. "Equal Job Opportunity Enforcement in Banks," 66 *L.R.R.* 51, 54 (10-2-67).

246. "FEP Moves by Banks, Government Contractors," 68 *L.R.R.* 320 (Vol. 68, No. 27, 8-15-68).

247. "FCC Adopts New Race-Bias Policy," 68 *L.R.R.* 257 (Vol. 68, No. 21, 7-15-68).

248. 29 U.S.C., Secs. 49 (b)-(n).

249. Mickel v. South Carolina State Employment Service Office, 377 F. 2d 239 (CA 4, 1967).

250. Many state commissions are not authorized to conduct investigations, but the EEOC does have investigatory power.

251. "Hiring and Seniority Under Title VII," 67 *L.R.R.* 378 (4-22-68).

252. *U.S. News & World Report*, pp. 40-44 (11-18-68).

253. Local 357, Teamsters Union v. NLRB, 365 U.S. 667 (1961).

254. Kerr v. Enoch Pratt Free Library, 149 F. 2d 212 (CA 4, 1945), *cert. denied*, 326 U.S. 721 (1945).

255. Marsh v. Alabama, 326 U.S. 501 (1946).

256. 334 U.S. 1 (1948).

257. Corrigan v. Buckley, 227 U.S. 323, 330 (1926); Queensborough Land Co. v. Cazeau, 136 La. 724, 67 So. 641 (1915); Los Angeles Investment Co. v. Gary, 181 Cal. 680, 186 P. 596 (1920).

258. Joseph and Barbara Jones v. Alfred H. Mayer Co., 379 F. 2d 33 (CA8, 1967). Actually, the issue in this case, whether the Fourteenth Amendment controlled, became moot when Congress passed Public Law 90-284; Section 804 calls for open housing.

259. This point is further developed starting at footnote 269.

260. 349 U.S. 70 (1955).

261. Spencer v. Flint Memorial Park Ass'n, 4 Mich. App. 157, 144 N.W. 2d 622 (1966).

262. 345 U.S. 461 (1953).

263. C. V. Woodward, *The Strange Career of Jim Crow*, pp. 128-129.

264. Ginzberg, *American Democracy and the Negro*, p. 11. Also see D. Parke Gibson, *The $30 Billion Dollar Negro Market* (1968).

265. Ross v. Ebert, 275 Wisc. 523, 82 N.W. 2d 315 (1957).

266. Ross v. Ebert, 82 N.W. 2d, at 320.

267. Barrows v. Jackson, 346 U.S. 249 (1953); Progress Development Corp. v. Mitchell, 286 F. 2d 222 (CA 7, 1961); Norris v. Mayor and City Council of Baltimore, 78 F. Supp. 451 (D. Md., 1948).

268. Todd v. Joint Apprenticeship Comm., 55 L.R.R.M. 2171 (N.D. Ill., 1963), reversed in part, 56 L.R.R.M. 2318 (CA 7, 1964).

269. Rice v. Sioux City Memorial Park Cemetery, 349 U.S. 70 (1955).

270. 365 U.S. 715 (1961).

271. 387 U.S. 369 (1967).

272. It is possible that laches may be invoked where the Fourteenth Amendment is resorted to because a statute of limitations outlaws the use of another remedy.

273. Bro. of R.R. Trainmen v. Howard, 343 U.S. 768 (1952); Tunstall v. Bro. of Locomotive Firemen, 323 U.S. 210 (1944); Steele v. Louisville and N.R.R., 323 U.S. 192 (1954); Conley v. Gibson, 355 U.S. 41 (1957); Syres v. Local 23, Oil Workers Union, 350 US.. 892 (1955). Many charge the railroad brotherhoods and lines with discrimination, but progress has been painfully slow.

274. See, for example, the *Report of the National Advisory Commission on Civil Disorders* (1968) and U.S. BUREAU OF LABOR STATISTICS, DEPT. OF LABOR, BULL. NO. 1511, *The Negroes in the United States* (1966).

275. U.S. BUREAU OF LABOR STATISTICS, DEPT. OF LABOR, BULL. NO. 1511, p. 25.

276. *Id.*, pp. 29, 35.

277. *Id.*, pp. 3, 41.

278. *Id.*, p. 28.

279. *Id.*, p. 24.

280. Fein, "An Economic and Social Profile of the Negro American," 94 *DAEDALUS* 816 (1965).

281. *Id.*, pp. 815-46.

282. *Ibid.*

283. U.S. BUREAU OF LABOR STATISTICS, DEPT. OF LABOR, BULL. NO. 1511, p. 25.

284. *Id.*, p. 27.

285. *Report of the National Advisory Commission on Civil Disorders*, p. 255.

286. Tobin, "On Improving the Economic Status of the Negro," 94 *DAEDALUS* 878-98 (1965).

287. Memorandum from Willard Wirtz, Secretary of Labor, *Validation of Employment Tests by Contractors and Subcontractors Subject to the Provisions of Executive Order 11246*, p. 2 (9-9-68).

288. *Commission Decision on Review*, Charge No. 63 C-127, State of Illinois F.E.P.C. (Nov. 18, 1964).

289. *Chicago Tribune*, Nov. 21, 1964, p. 14, col. 1; *Chicago American*, Nov. 23, 1964, p. 8, col. 1; *Chicago Daily News*, Nov. 23, 1964, p. 14, cols. 1-2; *Chicago Sun-Times*, Nov. 23, 1964 (editorial); Krock, "Fair Employment Issue, Decision in Illinois Case Involving Aptitude Test Raises Questions," *N.Y. Times*, Nov. 22, 1964, Sec. E, p. 9, col. 1.

290. Metzler and Kohrs, "Tests and 'The Requirements of the Job'," 20 *Arbitration Journal* 103 (1965).

291. B.N.A., *Daily Labor Report,* No. 81 (Monday, 4-28-69).

292. Motorola, Inc. v. Illinois F.E.P.C., 58 L.R.R.M. 2573, 2576 (1965).

293. 34 Ill. 2d 266, 281-282 (1966).

294. Ill. Ann. Stat., Ch. 48, sections 851, 867 (Smith-Hurd, 1961).

295. *Decision and Order of Hearing Examiner,* Charge No. 63C-177, at p. 10 (1964). Preference for the black was deemed undesirable in section 703 (j) of Title VII.

296. *Id.,* pp. 7-8.

297. Thompson v. Erie R.R., 2 *Race Rel. Law Rep.* 237 (1956); *Third Annual Report of the Ohio Civil Rights Commission,* pp. 21-22 (1962); Cooks v. Carmen's Local 338 F. 2d 59 (CA 5, 1964), *cert. denied,* 380 U.S. 975 (1965); City of Pittsburgh v. Plumbers Union, 59 L.R.R.M. 2553 (1965); Commission For Human Rights, 57 L.R.R.M. 2005 (N.Y. Sup. Ct., 1964).

298. Simpson and Yinger, *Racial and Cultural Minorities,* pp. 41-43; Lockwood, "Critical Problems in Achieving Equal Employment Opportunity," 19 *Personnel Psychology* 3, 8 (1966).

299. Allison, *Social-Class Influences Upon Learning,* pp. 2-3, 40-41 (1948); Cronbach, *Essentials of Psychological Testing,* p. 222 (1949); Thompson and Hughes, *Race Individual and Collective Behavior,* p. 223 (1958); Tiffin, *Industrial Psychology,* pp. 30, 75 (1943).

300. Educational Testing Services, *The Admission Test for Graduate Study in Business,* p. 71 (1966).

301. "EEOC Conciliation," 69 L.R.R. 275, 304 (Vol. 69, No. 25, 11-25-68). A black woman passed five out of six qualifying tests, but failed, by one point, an unvalidated test emphasizing verbal skills.

302. E.E.O.C., *Guidelines on Employment Testing Procedures,* p. 7 (1966). Subsequently referred to as *Guidelines.*

303. "Exam Questions Ruled Faulty," *Times-Democrat,* p. 12A, Column 2 (Davenport-Bettendorf, Iowa, 4-13-69). The New York Human Rights Commission found a civil service test discriminatory against black police officers seeking promotion because of the undue emphasis on grammar, which discriminates against the black with an inferior education.

304. Lockwood, "Employment Tests and Discriminatory Hiring," 5 *Industrial Relations* 20, 34-35 (Feb., 1966).

305. Matter of State Commission for Human Rights, 277 N.Y.S. 2d 287 (1967); affirmed, 19 N.Y. 2d 974 (1967).

306. Denniston, "Police Tests Assessed," *Washington Evening Star,* p. 14 (2-14-69).

307. "Workers Defense League Sets Patterns for Negro Job Gains," *AFL-CIO News,* p. 6 (2-8-69).

308. Grier and Cobbs, *Black Rage* (1968).

309. "Validity" is the accuracy with which a test measures what it is supposed to measure while "reliability" is the consistency with which the test does the job.

310. Metzler and Kohrs, "Tests and 'The Requirements of the Job'," 20 *Arbitration Journal* 103.

311. *Guidelines,* p. 3.

312. Prepared by American Psychological Association, American Education Research Association, and National Council on Measurement in Education (1966).

313. "Ruling on Bias in Testing Practices," 64 L.R.R. 31 (B.N.A. 1-16-67).

314. *Guidelines,* p. 4.

315. *Validation of Employment Tests by Contractors and Subcontractors Subject to the Provisions of Executive Order 11246,* Section 2 (a), p. 3 (9-9-68).

316. *Id.,* Section 6 (a), p. 7.

317. E. L. Kelly, *Assessment of Human Characteristics,* p. 87 (1967).

318. *Id.,* pp. 12-20; R. M. Allen, *Variables in Personality Theory and Personality Testing,* pp. 31-45 (1965).

319. The only solution may be to retest many times and take an average score.

320. "Ruling on Bias in Testing Practices," 64 L.R.R. 31 (Vol. 64, No. 5, 1-16-67).

321. Albright, Glennon and Smith, *The Use of Psychological Tests in Industry,* p. 17 (1963).

322. *Op. cit.*

323. Olmstead v. U.S., 277 U.S. 438, 478 (1928).

324. A. Westin, *Privacy and Freedom,* pp. 133-157 (1967). Also see *Torasco v. Watkins,* 367 U.S. 488 (1961), where a government test was administered to ferret out religious views.

325. "Apprenticeship Bias in 'Personal Trait' Grading," 67 L.R.R. 161, 164-165 (Vol. 67, No. 15, 2-19-68).

326. Lopez, "Current Problems in Test Performance of Job Applicants," 19 *Personnel Psychology* 10, 18 (1966).

327. *Guidelines,* pp. 3-4. Also see "New EEO Regulations for Government Contractors," 68 L.R.R. 103 (6-3-68).

328. *Id.,* p. 5.

329. 110 *Cong. Rec.* 12298 (daily edition, 6-4-64).

330. 42 U.S.C., Sec. 2000 e-5 (g).

331. NLRB v. Erie Resistor Corp., 373 U.S. 221, 227-228 (1963); Radio Officers Union v. NLRB, 347 U.S. 17, 44-45 (1954).

332. Motorola v. Illinois F.E.P.C., 34 Ill. 2d 266, 215 N.E. 2d 286. A similar problem arises under Illinois and federal law. The Illinois Commission must follow legal rules of evidence, while a court suit begins *de novo* under federal law.

333. Griggs v. Duke Power Co., 69 L.R.R.M. 2389 (U.S.D.C., M.D. N.C., 1968).

334. *Id.,* 2394.

335. B.N.A., "Two Agencies Invite Utilities to Meetings," *Daily Labor Report,* No. 107, p. 1 (5-31-68).

336. Metzler and Kohrs, "Tests and 'The Requirements of the Job'," 20 *Arbitration Journal,* p. 104.

337. McCormick, *Handbook of the Law of Evidence,* p. 640 (1954); Prosser, *Selected Topics on the Law of Torts,* pp. 302-309 (1953).

338. U.S. v. Aluminum Co. of America, 148 F. 2d 416 (1945).

339. 66 L.R.R.M. 2737 (U.S. Sup. Ct., 1967).

340. 388 U.S. 26 (1967).

341. F. James, *Civil Procedure,* Sec. 7.8, at p. 255 (1965).

342. *Id.,* at p. 257.

343. 49 Stat. 449 (1935).

344. Sayles, "Seniority: An Internal Union Problem," 30 *Harvard Business Review* 55 (1952).

345. Syres v. Oil Workers Union, 223 F. 2d 739 (CA5, 1955), affirmed, 350 U.S. 892 (1955).

346. Sec. 703 (h).

347. Harper v. Randolph, 56 L.R.R.M. 2130 (U.S.D.C., S.D.N.Y., 1964); Chicago Federation of Musicians, Local 10 v. American Fed. of Musicians, 57 L.R.R.M. 2227 (U.S.D.C., N.D. Ill., 1964).

348. Pellicer v. Bro. of Ry. & Steamship Clerks, 217 F. 2d 205 (CA 5, 1955), *cert. denied,* 349 U.S. 912 (1955); Holt v. Oil Workers Union, 36 L.R.R.M. 2702 (Texas Dist. Ct., 1955).

349. 45 U.S.C., Sec. 151 *et seq.*

350. 49 Stat. 449 (1935).

351. 28 U.S. Code, Sec. 151.

352. Syres v. Local 23, Oil Workers Union, 350 U.S. 892 (1955); Conley v. Gibson, 355 U.S. 41 (1957); Steele v. Louisville & N.R.R., 323 U.S. 192 (1954). In *Hughes Tool Co.,* 147 NLRB 1573 (1964), the NLRB resorted to the unfair labor practice provisions of the Taft-Hartley Act.

353. See Section 703 (j), Title VII, Civil Rights Act of 1964.

354. U.S. v. Local 189, Papermakers Union, 67 L.R.R.M. 2912 (U.S.D.C., E.D. La., 1968); Hicks v. Crown Zellerbach Corp., 69 L.R.R.M. 2005 (U.S.D.C., E.D. La., 1968).

355. Harper v. Randolph, 56 L.R.R.M. 2130 (U.S.D.C., S.D.N.Y., 1964).

356. U.S. v. H. K. Porter Co., 70 L.R.R.M. 2131 (U.S.D.C., N.D. Ala., 1968).

357. Secs. 8 (a) (5) and 8(b) (3).

358. NLRB v. Borg Warner, 356 U.S. 342 (1958).

359. Syres v. Oil Workers Union, 350 U.S. 892 (1955).

360. 110 Cong. Rec., p. 12297 (6-4-64).

361. Notes, "Title VII, Seniority Discrimination, and the Incumbent Negro." *80 Harvard Law Rev.* 1260, 1268 (1967).

362. Whitfield v. Steelworkers Union, 263 F. 2d 546 (CA5, 1959). *cert. denied,* 360 U.S. 902 (1959).

363. U.S. v. Local 189, Papermakers Union, 67 L.R.R.M. 2912 (U.S.D.C., E.D. La., 1968); Hicks v. Crown Zellerbach Corp., 69 L.R.R.M. 2005 (U.S.D.C., E.D. La., 1968).

364. Sec. 703 (c) (2).

365. Eleuterio v. Conley, 69 L.R.R.M. 2001 (U.S.D.C., S.D.N.Y., 1968).

366. Blue Bell Boats, Inc. v. E.E.O.C. 69 L.R.R.M. 2009 (U.S.D.C., M.D. Tenn., 1968); Georgia Power Co. v. E.E.O.C., 69 L.R.R.M. 2017 (U.S.D.C., N.D. Ga., 1968).

367. "EEOC Bid for Aid by Negro Press," 68 L.R.R. 199 (Vol. 68, No. 17, 7-1-08).

368. Fore v. Southern Bell Tel. Co., 69 L.R.R.M. 2631 (U.S.D.C., W.D., N.C., 1968); Stastny v. Southern Bell Tel. Co., 69 L.R.R.M. 2632 (U.S.D.C., W.D., N.C., 1968); Peurala v. U.S. Steel Corp., 68 L.R.R.M. 2979 (U.S.D.C., N.D., Ill., 1968); Hall v. Wertham Bag Co., 251 F. Supp. 184 (M.D. Tenn., 1966).

369. Pullen v. Otis Elevator Co., 68 L.R.R.M. 3015 (U.S.D.C., N.D. Ga., 1968).

370. *Id.,* 3016.

371. Carrington v. Douglas Aircraft Co., 69 L.R.R.M. 2654 (U.S.D.C., C.D. Calif., 1968).

372. Section 709 (e).

373. Johnson v. Seaboard Coast Line Rd. Co., 69 L.R.R.M. 2916 (CA 4, 1968). For similar decisions, see Mondy v. Crown Zellerbach, Hill v. Crown Zellerbach, 271 F. Supp. 258 (E.D. La., 1967); Edwards v. North American Rockwell Corp., 69 L.R.R.M. 2163 (U.S.D.C., C.D. Calif., 1968).

374. Evenson v. Northwest Airlines, 64 L.R.R.M. 2771 (U.S.D.C., F.D. Va., 1967).

375. Burrell v. Kaiser Aluminum Corp., 68 L.R.R.M. 3056 (U.S.D.C., E.D. La., 1968); Dent v. St. Louis-San Francisco Ry., 265 F. Supp. 56 (N.D. Ala., 1967); Reese v. Atlantic Steel Co., 67 L.R.R.M. 2475 (U.S.D.C., N.D. Ga., 1967); Miller v. Int. Paper Co., 67 L.R.R.M. 2790 (U.S.D.C., S.D. Miss., 1967); Anthony v. Brooks, 65 L.R.R.M. 3074 (N.D. Ga., 1967).

376. Rosen, "The Law and Racial Discrimination in Employment," 53 *Calif. Law Rev.* 729, 738 (1965).

149

377. Mickel v. So. Carolina State Employment Service, 377 F. 2d 239 (CA 4, 1967), *cert. denied*, 36 U.S. Law Week 3348 (1968).

378. Stebbins v. Nationwide Mutual Ins. Co., 382 F. 2d 267 (CA 4, 1967).

379. Bowe v. Colgate-Palmolive Co., 272 F. Supp. 332 (S. D. Ind., 1967); Hall v. Werthan Bag Corp., 251 F. Supp. 184 (M.D. Tenn., 1966).

380. U.S. v. Building and Construction Trades Council of St. Louis, 12 Race Relations Reporter 904 (U.S.D.C., St. Louis, Mo., 1966); Mondy v. Crown Zellerbach and Hill v. Crown Zellerbach, 271 F. Supp. 258 (E.D. La., 1967).

381. Textile Workers Union v. Lincoln Mills, 353 U.S. 448 (1957); Sinclair Refining Co. v. Atkinson, 370 U.S. 195 (1962).

382. Section 709 (d) pertaining to records also affects the federal-state relationship. This aspect is not considered herein.

383. See *E.E.O.C. v. Union Bank*, 69 L.R.R.M. 2417 (CA 9, 1968) where the charge was discrimination on the basis of sex. Also see *Washington v. Aerojet-General Corp.*, 67 L.R.R.M. 2959 (U.S.D.C., C.D., Calif., 1968); *Electrical Workers Union v. E.E.O.C.*, 65 L.R.R.M 3130 (US.D.C., W.D. Pa., 1967), *reversed* 68 L.R.R.M. 2939 (CA 3, 1968); *E.E.O.C. v. Local 780, Cement Masons Union*, 65 L.R.R.M. 2343 (U.S.D.C., S.D.N.Y., 1967); Edwards v. North American Rockwell Corp., 69 L.R.R.M. 2163 (U.S.D.C., C.D. Calif., 1968).

384. Dent. v. St. Louis-San Francisco Ry. Co., 265 F. Supp. 56 (N.D. La., 1967); Reese v. Atlantic Steel Co., 67 L.R.R.M. 2475 (U.S.D.C., N.D. Ga., 1967).

385. See Kovarsky, "The Negro and Fair Employment," 56 *Kentucky Law Journal*, 821-824. On January 14, 1969, in *Glover v. St. Louis-San Francisco Ry. Co.*, 70 L.R.R.M. 2097, the Supreme Court held that Negro employees facing discrimination in the railroad industry by employer and union need not, because it would be useless, first seek redress under a collective bargaining contract or petition the National Railroad Adjustment Board. No question was raised of invoking Title VII.

386. Smith v. Evening News, 371 U.S. 195 (1962). Racial discrimination was not an issue in this case. The availability of remedies was enlarged because the apparent unfair labor practice committed by the employer was also prohibited in the collective bargaining agreement.

387. Kovarsky, "The Negro and Fair Employment," 56 *Kentucky Law Journal*, 806-807.

388. Motorola, Inc. v. F.E.P.C., 34 Ill. 2d 266, 215 N.E. 2d 268 (1966); Amzie Waters, 9 *Race Rel. Law Rep.* 1522 (1964).

389. Steelworkers Union v. American Mfg. Co., 363 U.S. 564 (1960); Steelworkers Union v. Warrior and Gulf Navigation Co., 363 U.S. 574 (1960); Steelworkers Union v. Enterprise Wheel and Can Corp., 363 U.S. 593 (1960).

390. Dewey v. Reynolds Metals Co., 69 L.R.R.M. 2601 (W.D. Mich., 1968).

391. Edwards v. North American Rockwell Corp., 69 L.R.R.M. 2163 (U.S.D.C., C.D. Calif., 1968); Washington v. State Board Against Discrimination, 68 L.R.R.M. 2557 (Wash. Supreme Ct., 1968); Washington v. Aerojet-General Corp., 67 L.R.R.M. 2959 (U.S.D.C., C.D. Calif., 1968); Bowe v. Colgate-Palmolive Co., 65 L.R.R.M. 2714 (U.S.D.C., S.D. Ind., 1967).

392. 29 U.S.C., Sec. 141.

393. Raytheon Co., 52 L.R.R.M. 1129 (N.L.R.B., 1963); Spielberg Mfg. Co., 36 L.R.R.M. 1152 (N.L.R.B., 1955).

394. Labor Relations Reporter, S.L.L. 1:30-31 (1968).

395. Questionnaires were sent to all states with commissions. The information on the commissions contained in this section is based upon the replies received.

396. Only twenty-one states responded to this part of the questionnaire.

397. This includes 1967 data for two states for which 1968 data were not available.

398. U.S. Department of Health, Education, and Welfare, Office of Education, *Digest of Educational Statistics, 1968,* p. 107.

399. *Ibid.*

400. *MANPOWER REPORT OF THE PRESIDENT, 1969,* p. 85.

401. *GENERAL REPORT OF THE ADVISORY COUNCIL ON VOCATIONAL EDUCATION,* 1968, pp. 81-97.

402. *Id.,* pp. 81-97.

403. *Ibid.*

404. *HIGHLIGHTS AND RECOMMENDATIONS FROM THE GENERAL REPORT ON VOCATIONAL EDUCATION,* 1968, p. 36.

405. *Ibid.,* p. 37.

406. *MANPOWER REPORT OF THE PRESIDENT, 1969,* p. 86.

407. *Ibid.*

408. *Id.,* p. 76.

409. *Ibid.*

410. *Id.,* pp. 77, 78.

411. *Id.,* p. 77.

412. *Id.,* pp. 77, 78.

413. *Id.,* p. 78.

414. *Ibid.*

415. *Ibid.*

416. *Id.,* p. 79.

417. *Ibid.*

418. *Ibid.*

419. *Id.,* p. 89.

420. *Id.,* p. 90.

421. *Ibid.*

422. *Id.,* p. 91.

423. 69 L.R.R. 125, 69, 13 (1968).

424. *Ibid.*

425. Task Force on Occupational Training in Indsutry, *A Government Commitment to Occupational Training in Industry,* 50 (1968).

426. *MANPOWER REPORT OF THE PRESIDENT, 1969,* pp. 219-22.

427. *Id.,* p. 93.

428. *Id.,* p. 94.

429. *Ibid.*

430. *Id.,* p. 100.

431. *Id.,* pp. 100, 101.

432. *Id.,* p. 101.

433. *Id.,* p. 98.

434. *Id.,* pp. 98, 99.

435. *Id.,* p. 99.

436. *Ibid.*

437. *Ibid.*

438. *Ibid.*

439. *Id.,* pp. 102, 103.

440. *Id.,* p. 104.

441. *Id.,* pp. 104, 105.

442. *Id.,* p. 105.

443. *Id.,* p. 106.

444. *Ibid.*
445. *Id.,* pp. 125, 126.
446. *Id.,* pp. 132, 133.
447. *Id.,* p. 133.
448. *Id.,* p. 134.
449. *Id.,* pp. 134, 135.
450. *Id.,* pp. 135, 136.
451. B. Bettleheim and M. Janovitz, *Social Change and Prejudice,* p. 15 (1964).